The Mercedes-Benz since 1945
Volume 1

The Mercedes-Benz since 1945

Volume 1: The 1940s and 1950s

A collector's guide
by James Taylor

MOTOR RACING PUBLICATIONS LTD
32 Devonshire Road, Chiswick, London W4 2HD, England

ISBN 0 900549 95 5
First published 1985

Photosetting by Tek-Art Ltd, West Wickham, Kent
Printed in Great Britain by The Garden City Press Ltd, Letchworth, Hertfordshire SG6 1JS

Contents

Introduction and acknowledgements

I have always liked Mercedes-Benz cars; indeed, it would surprise me to find any motoring enthusiast who did not number at least one of the company's products among his all-time favourites. All the more galling, then, to find not a single book among the scores available in the English language which actually sets out the factual history of those cars and describes their development and production history in detail. I have read plenty of well-written books of superficial or subjective impressions, several more crammed full of inaccuracies, and just a few which deal admirably with a single aspect of Mercedes-Benz history – but not one which answered all the questions I had. So, rushing in where angels have clearly feared to tread, I decided to write such a book myself.

The first thing which struck me about this task was the immense complexity of Mercedes-Benz model history – hence my work is divided into three Volumes, of which this is only the first. The second thing which rapidly became apparent was that to write a detailed history of every model ever made by the oldest car manufacturer in the world might be a lifetime's occupation. As such things as publisher's deadlines tend to intrude on that blissful twilight world of late evenings spent among piles of old motoring magazines and photographs, I decided to write only about those cars built by Daimler-Benz since the end of the Second World War. This is the period, I think, for which there is currently the most widespread interest among enthusiasts.

With such lofty aims, it will be surprising indeed if I have not fallen short of the mark on more than one occasion in the pages which follow. Nonetheless, things would undoubtedly have been much worse were it not for the kind help I have had from Poul Jørgensen and Colin Peck in checking through portions of the text. The same pair also contributed a number of photographs to this volume, drawn from their private collections.

Facts, photographs and help in general came also from several members of the enthusiasts' clubs, both in this country and in the USA, and I am most grateful for their assistance. The National Motor Museum at Beaulieu was, as ever, an invaluable reference source, and has also provided certain photographs. Even Anders Clausager, at the British Motor Industry Heritage Trust, was able to help out with photographs!

I owe a further debt of gratitude to Rainer Karnowski, at the Daimler-Benz historical archives in Stuttgart, who kindly sought out a good deal of material. Finally, thanks go to my editor/publisher John Blunsden – who at one stage was thinking of writing this book himself – and to my dear wife Lesley Ann, who has not only tolerated my periods of unavailability while this book was being written, but has also contributed several photographs to it, including that on the cover.

JAMES L. TAYLOR

Woodcote, Oxfordshire
January 1985

Note: Mercedes-Benz works designations need a word or two of explanation. Design numbers are allocated to both engines and complete vehicles, and these numbers are preceded by an identifying letter: W (for Wagen) on road and racing cars alike, M (for Motor) on petrol engines, and OM (for Ölmotor) on diesel engines. Infuriatingly, there is no consistent logic or chronology about the allocation of these design numbers, and cars as similar as the 170S and 170DS bear different numbers, whilst models as dissimilar as the 190 saloon and the 190SL sports car bear the same design number! A similar lack of consistent logic is found in the type-designations, where the S of 170S stands for 'Super', while in 300SL it stands for 'Sports'; and as for 300S, it could mean either!

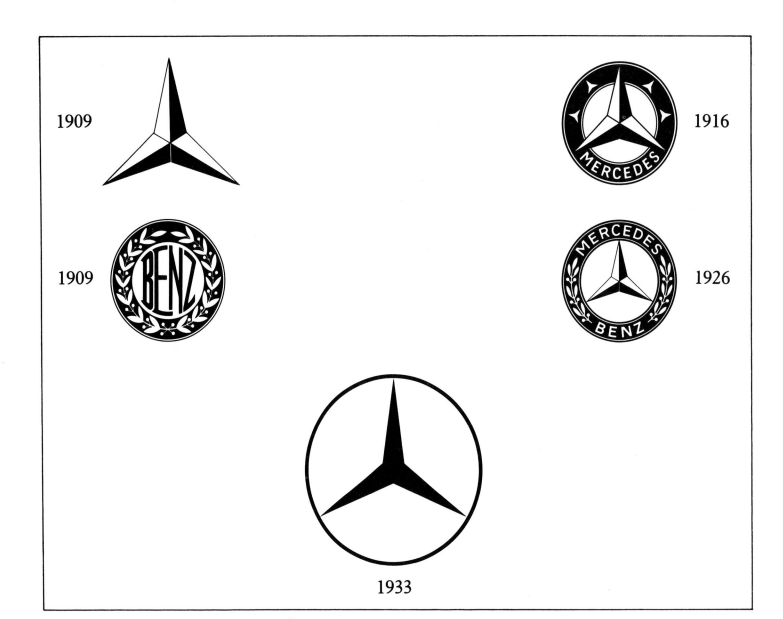

1909

1916

1909

1926

1933

CHAPTER 1

Ancestors and parentage

The Daimler and Benz family tree

Germany's most famous motor vehicle manufacturer really came into being as a result of the dramatic inflation which gripped the country after 1923, although its component parts had been in existence for nearly 40 years before that. Benz und Cie, of Mannheim, and the Daimler Motorengesellschaft, based a little further south in the Untertürkheim district of Stuttgart, had by the early 1920s achieved undisputed joint domination of the German motor industry, but it rapidly became clear that both would not survive the Recession. Swallowing their pride with an ease not normally associated with the Teutonic race, they decided that co-operation would best ensure their future. The two companies began working together in 1924, and within two years they had merged to become the Daimler-Benz Aktiengesellschaft.

Not only did the constituent parts of the new company represent Germany's leading motor manufacturers, but both had played enormously important parts in the development of the motor car. Karl Benz had worked as a young man for a Stuttgart carriage-builder, but the burgeoning gas engine industry tempted him to design his own two-stroke stationary engine, and he moved into that industry to work for the Gasmotorenfabrik Mannheim AG, a modest stationary engine enterprise. His next step was to secure financial backing and to set up on his own in the stationary engine business as Benz und Cie, Rheinische Gasmotorenfabrik, in 1883.

Yet while gas engines provided his bread and butter, Benz was interested in combining his knowledge of the carriage trade with his expertise in building stationary engines, and producing a self-propelled vehicle. Turning for fuel to petrol – which was then used mainly as a cleaning agent – he designed a water-cooled four-stroke engine which he installed in a three-seater vehicle which first ran in 1885. This vehicle is generally considered to have been the world's first motor car.

At this stage, of course, there was no real market for motorized transport, and so Benz continued experimenting and refining his invention until sufficient interest had been generated for him to consider seriously going into the production of motor cars. Limited production began in 1890, alongside the company's gas engines, and the business began to gather momentum rapidly. Benz was joined that year by two partners, who relieved him of the responsibility for sales and administration, leaving him free to deal with technical innovation. He was able to progress rapidly from his original three-wheel designs to a four-wheeler called the Viktoria in 1891, and four years later he developed a van and bus from the basic design. Meanwhile, the technical advances of the expensive Viktoria had been adapted to a much cheaper model known as the Velo and introduced in 1894. This was the world's first series-production car.

Production figures in those days were, of course, laughably small by modern standards, but Benz continued to introduce new models in the later 1890s and by the end of the decade he had built 2,000 cars and had a production capacity of 600 cars a year. In addition, he had sales agencies in several far-flung countries. All this was sufficient to make the Benz company the world's leading motor manufacturer at the turn of the century. Yet Benz himself was a man of conservative disposition, not at all keen to mass-produce his designs or make constant changes

Where it all began. Karl Benz's 1886 three-wheeler, which was powered by a single-cylinder 984cc engine producing 0.9bhp at 400rpm. It was shown to the public for the first time at Mannheim on July 3 that year, when speeds up to 15km/h (9mph) were reached.

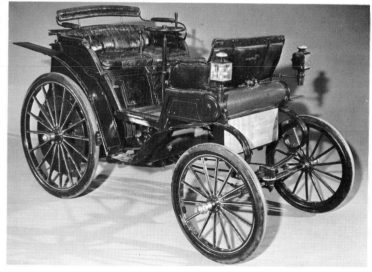

An early offering from Daimler. This vis-à-vis dates from 1894 and was driven by a twin-cylinder engine of just over 1-litre displacement which delivered 3.5bhp at 720rpm, giving the vehicle a speed of around 25km/h (15mph).

to them, and above all opposed to any association with motor sport, even though it was this which attracted the customers he needed. The Benz designs rapidly became outdated as motor car development began to make progress by leaps and bounds, and sales began to slump. In desperation, Benz's sales director engaged another designer to build a new model using the modern shaft-drive instead of the belt-drive favoured by Benz himself. This went on sale in 1902, but it was hardly a success. Karl Benz was furious, and left his own company a year later. He was persuaded to rejoin briefly in 1905 – and helped the ailing company to get back on its feet – but in 1906 he left for good.

This left the old Benz company under the guidance of its chief engineer, Hans Nibel, who astutely recognized that the quickest way of getting the company back onto equal footing with its arch-rivals at Daimler was to go in for racing. Nibel persuaded his Board to allocate the necessary funds, and the comeback began in 1907. By 1909 Benz had made sufficient technical progress to produce the streamlined Blitzen-Benz, a 200bhp

Pride of achievement is personified by the facial expressions provided for this posed picture of a Benz vis-à-vis in 1891. The company had begun limited production of horseless carriages the previous year after several years of experimentation with prototypes.

21½-litre monster which made mincemeat of the racing opposition and held the World Land Speed Record until 1922, after first breaking it in 1909. Of such stuff are legends made, and Benz profited accordingly.

In the last years before the First World War, the Benz company introduced a wide range of road cars, which sold to an increasingly broad market, and in 1914 they introduced their first six-cylinder model. Wartime saw the inevitable concentration on trucks and aero-engines, but when peace returned the Benz company faced problems. Germany's economy had been shattered, and the market was slow to pick up. Although there were brave attempts at publicity through racing – notably the Tropfenwagen teardrop-shaped car with rear-mounted engine of 1923 – the road cars were mainly conventional vehicles derived from a 1914 design. Important developments were nevertheless being made: the Tropfenwagen, for example, bore swing-axle suspension, while

in 1922 there appeared a diesel engine for Benz Sendling tractors, which incorporated a precombustion chamber. These innovations would have a marked effect on the future Mercedes-Benz.

Like Karl Benz, Gottfried Daimler came from the stationary engine industry in Germany. He was a specialist in internal combustion engines, and more particularly in the four-stroke type built by the company of which he was chief engineer, the Gasmotorenfabrik Deutz, which had been founded by Nikolaus August Otto, after whom the four-stroke 'Otto cycle' is still known. Deutz was a prosperous company and was anxious to become even more so by streamlining production, but Daimler was more interested in improving and refining the product than in simply mass-producing existing designs. The difference of views came to a head in 1882 when Daimler decided to resign from the company and to set up his own experimental workshop in Bad Cannstatt.

Bodywork had developed from the horseless-carriage style towards more logical lines for motorized transport by 1902, when this Mercedes Simplex made its debut. Powered by a four-cylinder 5.3-litre engine producing 32bhp at 1,100rpm, the car had a top speed of just over 37mph.

Free to experiment as he wished, and accompanied by the brilliant Wilhelm Maybach, whom he had also lured away from Deutz, Daimler set to work on the design of high-speed internal combustion engines suitable for use in boats, trains, or road vehicles. By 1883 he had produced the world's first petrol-powered internal combustion engine, and after a series of trials with a motorcycle, a boat and a sleigh, it was in 1886 – one year later than Karl Benz's first three-wheeler – that he put his engine into a suitably modified horse-drawn carriage.

This was Daimler's first car, although he did not set up formally as a motor car manufacturer until 1890, and the first Daimler car produced in any numbers was not introduced until 1895. It was in fact Maybach who had pushed the rather conservative Daimler into car manufacture, finally persuading him that a car should be designed as such from first principles, and not simply adapted from a horse-drawn vehicle. The Stahlradwagen of 1889, so nicknamed because of its steel wire wheels, was just such a design, a four-wheeled two-seater with a tubular steel frame and its V-twin engine mounted at the rear.

Daimler and Maybach showed it at the 1889 Paris World Fair, where it attracted great interest and – more significantly in commercial terms – requests for licensing agreements from several French companies to build the Daimler engine. Among these were Peugeot and Panhard-Levassor, who effectively founded the French car industry as they signed their licensing agreements.

By the close of the 1880s, then, the Daimler Motorengesellschaft was a thriving concern. Sales of its marine engines alone were huge, and the company even had its own shipyard for building the tugs into which these engines were put. Yet the Board was keen to increase production at the expense of research, and Daimler once again found himself out on a limb. In 1893 he left the company with Maybach in order to continue his experiments. The business, however, slumped, and two years later Daimler and Maybach were persuaded to return, bringing with them the important innovation of the atomizing carburettor. 1895 saw the introduction of a belt-driven two-cylinder car, succeeded in 1897 by the Phönix,

Between 1904 and 1907 a small number of cars were built under licence from Daimler in Long Island City, USA. This is a 1906 45hp Mercedes, which was identical except in small details to the German-built equivalent.

which was the firm's first front-engined design; and then two years later appeared the first four-cylinder Daimler.

At this point, Emil Jellinek enters the Daimler story. A wealthy motoring enthusiast, he was also Consul-General of the Austro-Hungarian Empire in Nice, and operated as an unofficial Daimler agent selling the firm's cars to his equally wealthy friends. In 1900 he was elected to the Daimler Board, and proposed that the company should attract publicity and sales by building a completely new high-performance car. So Wilhelm Maybach – without Daimler himself, who had died that year – set to work to design a 35hp, four-cylinder, 5.9-litre car incorporating certain features of the PD car designed by Gottfried Daimler's son Paul. The result was probably the first 'real' car, with a host of technical innovations and an appearance

which owed absolutely nothing to the horse-drawn carriage. The first one was seen at the Nice Week motoring trials in 1901, and before long its design was being copied all over Europe and America.

Like the 28hp Daimler which Jellinek had entered for the 1899 Nice Week trials, the 35hp car was entered under the pseudonym Mercédès, the name of Jellinek's eldest daughter. Jellinek, meanwhile, was actively negotiating for the sole agency for Daimler cars in the Austro-Hungarian Empire, in the USA, in Belgium, and in France. To overcome legal difficulties with Panhard-Levassor, who pointed out that they held the licence to build Daimler engines in France, he agreed to market the cars under the name Mercedes rather than Daimler. The sales and racing successes of the cars called Mercedes were such that in

13

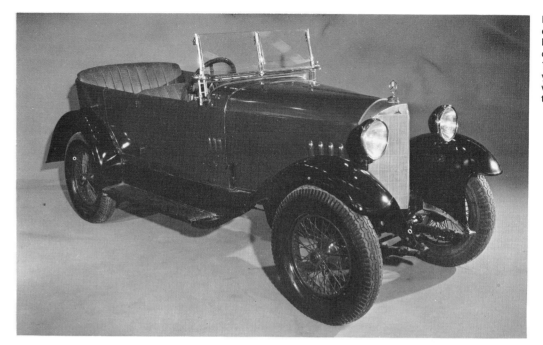

Benefiting from their aero-engine experience during the First World War, Daimler were able to offer a production car with a supercharged engine from 1921. This is the 6/25/40PS model of that year, the four-cylinder 1,568cc engine of which was boosted from 25 to 40bhp by the addition of the blower.

1902 the Daimler Board decided to adopt the name, without the accents, for all the company's private cars.

The 35hp car of 1901 spawned a whole range of Mercedes tourers and racing cars, which earned the Daimler company a reputation for building elegant vehicles which appealed to Royalty and to the merely rich alike, while initiating what was to be a long and distinguished career on the race tracks. Yet there were changes in the wind: in 1907 Maybach left the company to set up on his own, and Jellinek resigned from the Board the following year after returning his agency licences in 1905. The new chief engineer was Daimler's son Paul, who returned to the company after a spell with Austro-Daimler (the company's Austrian branch), and from 1908 the lighter Mercedes models dispensed with their traditional chain-drive in favour of shaft-drive. In the meantime, the MMB factory at Marienfelde, in Berlin, which had been established by a former Daimler company director to produce cars under the Daimler name, had

been bought out and equipped as a commercial vehicle plant. Similar diversification was evident in the production by the main company during 1906-07 of electric cars made under licence from Austro-Daimler.

1909 saw the arrival of Knight engines, again built under licence, which formed the backbone of the Mercedes car range until 1924. The three-pointed star was registered in 1911 as the company's trademark; but then came the First World War. The Daimler factories were turned over to the production of, amongst other things, supercharged aero engines; and not surprisingly the associated technology was put to good use after the war in Mercedes cars. The first production cars with a Roots-type blower were exhibited at the 1921 Berlin Motor Show. Yet there were more changes just around the corner. Paul Daimler retired as chief engineer in 1922, to be succeeded by Ferdinand Porsche, another former Austro-Daimler man; and it was by now clear that Germany's two biggest car makers could

At the time Daimler were introducing their first supercharged Mercedes car, Benz were offering this 6/18 model, the 1.57-litre engine of which was claimed to produce 45bhp at 3,200rpm. The two companies were direct competitors in a considerable area of the market, and a future merger was already looking inevitable.

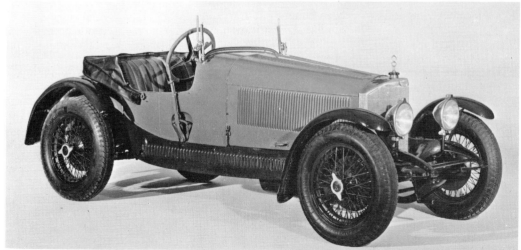

The supercharged version of the 10/40/65 Mercedes was one of the exhibits in a display at the 1974 Geneva Motor Show assembled to celebrate the exhibition's 50th anniversary, this 1924 car having been one of the models on view at the inaugural event.

15

The famous Mercedes-Benz SSKL from 1930, a car which had evolved from the SSK series and which, like its predecessor, was to quickly establish an enviable reputation in competitions. Its six-cylinder 7,069cc engine produced 300bhp at 3,400rpm in supercharged form.

A very dignified and formal model, the 1926 Mannheim was one of the first joint Mercedes-Benz products. Designated a 12/55, it had a six-cylinder 2,968cc engine which developed 55bhp at 3,500rpm.

The Mercedes-Benz range was moved further up-market in 1930 with the introduction of the 770, otherwise known as the Grosser Mercedes, a series of cars of impressive dimensions, an eight-cylinder 7,655cc engine and a wide range of specialist bodywork including this four-door cabriolet with extended luggage trunk.

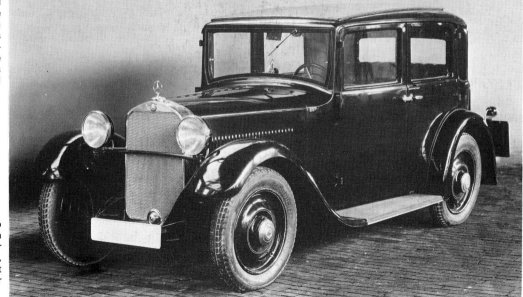

The following year the company also extended their range down-market with the type 170, featuring a six-cylinder 1,692cc engine developing 32bhp, transverse-leaf independent front suspension and swing-axle rear suspension.

17

The swing-axle rear-end of the Mercedes-Benz 170, which employed dual vertical coil springs beneath the upswept channel-section chassis-frame.

not both survive the postwar recession. So in 1924, the first steps towards a co-operative merger of the Daimler and Benz companies were made, and by 1926 the Daimler-Benz Aktiengesellschaft had become a fully-integrated whole, with its cars being marketed under the three-pointed star of Mercedes, surrounded by the laurel wreath of Benz. The cars bore a new name – Mercedes-Benz.

After the merger, the supercharged Mercedes models continued in production alongside the 16/50PS Benz, but the results of the pre-merger collaboration appeared as early as 1926 when the 2-litre Stuttgart and 3.1-litre Mannheim models appeared, each named after the town where it was built. These were conventional chassis designed to bear conventional saloon bodies, but Porsche, who had become chief engineer of the new combine, had no intention of letting Mercedes-Benz cars be bogged down by convention. For 1926 he revised the 24/100 Mercedes model derived from Paul Daimler's prewar designs, giving its 6-litre supercharged engine an extra quarter-litre of

displacement and shortening the wheelbase to reduce weight. The new car was launched under the designation K (for Kurz, or short, although in later times the K would stand for Kompressor, or supercharger), and thus began a whole line of what are now legendary high-performance sports/racing cars, which kept the Mercedes-Benz name in the public eye, even though the economic gloom had forced the company to withdraw temporarily from Grand Prix racing.

No matter how deep the economic depression in an industrialized country, there always remains a market for luxury goods of the highest quality and cost. The K sold on the strength of its desirability as the fastest touring car of its time in the world, and from it were derived in turn the 6.8-litre S in 1927 and the 7.1-litre SS and short-chassis SSKL of 1928. Of course, these models sold in very limited numbers, and such money as Mercedes-Benz cars were bringing in during those dark years came from the more mundane products. Yet even these bore witness to chief engineer Porsche's interest in speed, for the Stuttgart saloon was given a larger engine to become the Stuttgart 260, and the Mannheim turned into a 3½-litre Mannheim 350, thus inaugurating the Mercedes-Benz tradition of a three-figure type-number directly related to the cubic capacity of the engine.

The 1930s represented a Golden Age for Mercedes-Benz, when the company's engineering prowess reached its zenith. It was able to build on the glamour of the fabulous sports tourers whose line had been initiated by Porsche's K model in 1926; it re-entered international racing in 1934 after a lay-off period caused by Germany's severe economic depression; and the engineering advances which went into these cars led to exciting developments in the more mundane road cars as well as to a formidable amount of publicity and a great enhancement of the Mercedes-Benz reputation.

The 1930s opened with Hans Nibel as chief engineer, having taken over from Porsche in 1928 when the latter had left the company to pursue his own visions. Porsche was a hard act to follow but, undaunted, Nibel oversaw the development of the sports/racing SSKL successor to Porsche's high-performance line, a truly incredible machine with a lightened chassis and a huge supercharger, one streamlined example of which achieved a 156mph top speed. This, however, was really a development

The 1933 Mercedes-Benz 380 with supercharged eight-cylinder 3,820cc engine producing 140bhp at 3,600rpm. This four-door sports-saloon body was one of several styles offered on this chassis.

The 290 range, powered by a 60bhp six-cylinder engine, was introduced in 1933, to be followed a year later by this longer-wheelbase version, which again was offered with a variety of bodywork styles. The 290 remained in production until 1937.

Odd men out in the Mercedes-Benz range in the 1930s were the 150 Heckmotor models with their rear-mounted 1,498cc four-cylinder engines. This two-seater sports-roadster was perhaps the most dramatic-looking of the range and was not unlike a contemporary Adler in appearance.

of the Porsche design, and Nibel's own taste lay in rather more elegant and less overtly sporting machinery. Moreover, he was a chassis and suspension specialist, where Porsche had been an engines man, and so when the SSKL was superseded in 1933 by the supercharged 380, the new car was seen to have swing-axle suspension for the first time on a Mercedes-Benz sports car. Yet Nibel's hour of triumph did not come until a year later, when the first of the really great Mercedes-Benz road cars of the 1930s was introduced. This was the 500K, with an enlarged version of the 380's engine, which gave a top speed of over 100mph when fitted with the optional supercharger. Compared with an SSKL, this was perhaps not an earth-shattering speed, but the 500K was a ridiculously fast car for its time and – more important – it was usually fitted with expensive and good-looking coachbuilt bodies, which meant that it was luxurious as well.

Sales convinced Daimler-Benz that the 500K was the way to go, even though the very nature of such machines meant that they would be produced in small numbers. In 1936, the 500K was succeeded by the 100mph 540K with a supercharger as standard attachment to its 5.4-litre straight-eight engine.

Without any doubt, the 540K with its Mercedes-built two-seater roadster body was one of the most extravagantly elegant cars of its time; and it is still a much sought-after 'classic' today.

In the same year which saw the introduction of the 500K model, the Daimler-Benz company once again entered the world of international racing which, since their retirement some eight years earlier, had been dominated by the Italians. Their first effort was the W25 car, a supercharged eight-cylinder machine of 3.36 litres and some 354bhp, which had been carefully designed to fit into the 750-kilogramme maximum-weight formula dreamed up for the 1934 season by the *Association Internationale des Automobile-Clubs* (AIAC). The W25 completely outshone all the competition in its very first race at the Nürburgring on June 3, 1934, and thus began a period of six years during which the Mercedes-Benz works team reigned supreme in international motor racing. The W25 was further developed for 1937 into the W125, with a 550bhp engine of 5.6 litres, which gave it a 211mph capability with the right gearing. A streamlined version of the car built specifically as a record-breaker actually attained 380mph. So far ahead of their rivals were the Mercedes-Benz Grand Prix cars that the AIAC was forced in 1938 to introduce a new racing formula, limiting the size of supercharged engines to 3 litres and establishing a minimum weight limit of 850 kilogrammes.

Undeterred, the Daimler-Benz racing department under Alfred Neubauer set to work to build a winner within the new formula and came up with not one, but two designs. The W154 and W163 Grand Prix cars were powered by a supercharged 2,962cc V12 engine, which put out over 480bhp. Throughout the 1938 and 1939 seasons, the familiar names of the Mercedes-Benz works drivers – Lang, Caracciola, von Brauchitsch and Seaman – racked up victory after victory, often turning in 'Mercedes trademark' results of first, second and third placings. Yet this sort of success story made Daimler-Benz few friends in the racing fraternity, and for 1939 the Italians succeeded in arranging a very late change to the formula rules for the Tripoli Grand Prix. With less than eight months to go, the Mercedes-Benz team were obliged to develop a racer to fit into the 1½-litre class in which Alfa-Romeo and Maserati already had some tried and tested vehicles. With all hands on deck, the racing department came up with the little W165, a 1½-litre V8 car which raced only the once before war put a stop to international motor racing – and the two cars entered came first and second, much to the annoyance of the Italians.

The Daimler-Benz philosophy was, and still is, that motor racing has a deeper purpose than mere publicity. That purpose is to stretch engineering development to the limit and thus to provide the spur for better engineering in the road-going cars. The first new family car produced under Hans Nibel's reign was eloquent testimony to this philosophy: the 1931 170 model used the swing-axle independent suspension which Nibel had first fitted to the 1923 racer he had helped build for his employers at Benz. Swing-axles again appeared in the 1933 290 model, although the independent front suspension was still of a rather crude type with twin transverse leaf springs; and for 1936 the old box-section frames were superseded on the smaller saloons by a new backbone-type cruciform chassis of oval tubes. The first cars to bear this were a completely-revised 170 model (now known as a 170V) and the bigger 230.

Nibel's interest in backbone-type chassis also manifested

The 170V first entered the Mercedes-Benz catalogue as a 1936 model and it quickly established itself as the company's most popular model, nearly 72,000 examples being produced before the Second World War brought production to a halt. This was the car which was to help put the company back on the car manufacturing map once hostilities had ceased.

itself in the one unsuccessful range of cars which came from the Mercedes-Benz stable in the 1930s. This was a range of cars with small-capacity, rear-mounted engines, which had been under development at Daimler-Benz since Porsche's time in 1927, and were the true forerunners of his later 'People's Car' design, which is better known as the Volkswagen Beetle. The first one was the 130H, and appeared in 1933. An open sports two-seater with a larger engine and the 150H designation appeared the following year, and a 1.7-litre version known as the 170H was launched for 1936 (the H stood for Heckmotor – rear engine – and explains why the conventional 170 became a 170V in 1936, the V standing for Vorn – front – and indicating engine position). Yet the Heckmotor saloons were never very successful in sales terms.

Tremendously successful, however, was the world's first diesel-engined car, which Mercedes-Benz introduced in 1936. Diesel engines had, of course, been part of the Daimler-Benz stock-in-trade since their introduction in that agricultural tractor in 1922, but problems of vibration and size had effectively confined their use to commercial vehicles since then.

By 1932, problems of downsizing had been overcome, but vibration was still a problem and the original plan to introduce a diesel-engined passenger car that year was shelved. Four years later, however, Daimler-Benz triumphantly introduced the 260D, a medium-sized saloon with a distinctly modest performance, but the formidable economy and longevity of the diesel engine. It had originally been intended for use mainly as a taxi in saloon form, and there was talk of introducing light commercial versions, such as vans. In the event, however, the saloon's popularity with the ordinary motorist ruled out all thoughts of introducing additional models, and the 260D remained a strong seller right up until the war.

One further vehicle from the Mercedes-Benz Golden Age deserves consideration here, for it represented the beginnings of a tradition which continued in the Mercedes-Benz range until the early 1980s. This was the Grosser model, a huge luxury limousine introduced in 1930 and given respectable performance despite its great weight by a 150bhp, 7.7-litre derivative of Porsche's 7.1-litre straight-eight engine, which produced no fewer than 200bhp with its supercharger engaged.

One of the most spectacular-looking Mercedes-Benz cars in the late 1930s was the two-seater roadster version of the 540K series introduced as a 1937 model and powered by an eight-cylinder engine producing up to 180bhp in supercharged form.

During the 1930s there was a progressive move away from traditional channel-section steel chassis towards oval-tube structures, some of them in X-formation. This is the type 230 rolling chassis, introduced at the end of 1938. Note the leaf-spring front and coil-spring and swing-axle rear independent suspension layouts.

Clearly intended for State occasions, the ultimate in high performance and luxury is suggested by this cabriolet F version of the 1939 type 770 Grosser Mercedes, with accommodation for seven or eight passengers and power from an eight-cylinder 7,655cc engine with either a single or twin superchargers.

The Grosser was a car intended for Royalty, and it was built in very limited numbers. Seven were ordered by the household of the Emperor of Japan, and three remain in use for ceremonial occasions to this day. Production ran out in 1937, by which time the Grosser had become the last Mercedes-Benz saloon to use the old box-section type frame. It was replaced for 1938 by the 770K model, which used a slightly uprated version of the same engine, giving 155bhp without the blower and 230 bhp on full boost, and had rather more modern body styling on the new cruciform backbone frame, and swing-axle suspension. The vast 770K was capable of over 100mph, but earned itself a most unfortunate reputation when senior Nazi Party members adopted it as their official vehicle. It continued in production until the outbreak of war, at which time there were plans to replace the blown 7.7-litre engine by a 6-litre derivative of the V12 engine from the Grand Prix cars.

The war, of course, changed everything. An industrial concern with the resources and ability of the Daimler-Benz Aktiengesellschaft could not avoid being drawn into Germany's war effort, and for the six years from 1939 the company's factories were devoted to the manufacture of trucks, tanks, airframes and aero engines. Car production stopped altogether in 1942, by which time the only passenger car remaining in production was a derivative of the four-cylinder 170V saloon, which ran on wood-gas and was known as the 170VG. There can be no denying that the Mercedes-Benz products of these years – especially the aero-engines – maintained the extremely high standards which the company had set during the previous decade, and it was not at all surprising that the Allies should have singled out the Daimler-Benz factories for special treatment. In the autumn of 1944, with the tide of the war turning and Germany falling back on the defensive, Allied bombing raids pounded the factories at Stuttgart to rubble. The industrial concern which had once held its head so high was totally and utterly destroyed. A statement issued by the Daimler-Benz Board of Directors in 1945 made no bones about the damage: 'At this point, ' it said, 'the company had practically ceased to exist'.

CHAPTER 2

A phoenix from the ashes

The 170 and 220 models

It is difficult now even to conceive of the utter demoralization and despair into which the German nation was pitched after the signing of an unconditional surrender on May 7, 1945, and the pessimism of the Daimler-Benz directors is symptomatic of this as much as of the terrible losses sustained by the company. All must have seemed to them quite lost: quite apart from the destruction of their factories, the different plants were now spread across three of the military occupation zones, with Untertürkheim, Sindelfingen and Mannheim under American control, Gaggenau isolated in the French sector, and Marienfelde rapidly being denuded in the name of war reparations by the Russians, into whose hands it had fallen. When Untertürkheim re-opened its gates one month to the day after the final bombing raid, it admitted not the 20,000 employees of its heyday, but a skeleton workforce of 1,240 who were permitted under the watchful eye of the American troops to do no more than begin the work of clearing the debris and salvaging what they could.

Although the occupying powers had no intention of allowing Germany to re-establish its former industrial might, they recognized that the appalling conditions of the postwar nation could only be alleviated if it was permitted to get back onto a sound economic footing. This meant that some kind of industrial life had to start again, and so when the Daimler-Benz workforce had salvaged what remained of the company's plant and machinery, it was permitted to keep itself busy by undertaking repair and maintenance work on existing vehicles. Meanwhile, work began on rebuilding the factories, and bit by bit some of the old company pride began to return. Despite the

difficult winter of 1945-46, when the factories were denied coal, gas and electricity, by the middle of the following year reconstruction had reached the stage where it was possible to contemplate the limited production of motor vehicles once again.

Miraculously, the production lines for the 170V saloon, which had lain idle since 1942, had survived the bombing. These and such parts stocks as had survived were moved into the Untertürkheim factory, and the Daimler-Benz directors gained permission from the American Military Commander to start production again alongside the repair and maintenance work. Obviously, this production had to be very limited: there was the simple fact that raw materials were in short supply; there was the limiting factor that in 1946 living conditions were so bad that most Germans were more worried about where their next meal was coming from than what new cars were available; and of course the occupying powers had agreed in March that year that German industrial output should not be allowed to exceed roughly half of its 1938 level. So Daimler-Benz were initially permitted to build only such vehicles as might be of direct benefit to the nation's social and economic recovery. The production of private cars did not fall into this category, and so the first postwar 170V models to appear were delivery vans, pick-up trucks, or ambulances.

Gradually, things became a little better. The draconian regulations enforced by the occupying Allies relaxed, and by May 1947 Daimler-Benz was permitted once again to indulge in the luxury of building cars. Of course, these had to be 170V models, for there had been neither time nor finance to develop

Permission to resume manufacture after the Second World War was initially conditional on the production of utilitarian vehicles for essential use, such as this neat pick-up, based on the 170V chassis.

anything new, and as the market could still not take exotica such as the pretty little two-door cabriolets of the prewar years, the only model available was the four-door saloon. Nevertheless, this was a start, and Daimler-Benz determined to build on it.

1947: The 170V

The postwar 170V differed from its prewar counterpart mainly in the sometimes doubtful quality of its construction, which in all fairness was not the fault of its manufacturers, but of their difficulties in obtaining raw materials. It was outwardly a typical late 1930s design, with an upright radiator grille flanked by exposed headlamps, sweeping front wings and running-boards which terminated in a short, neat, rear wing. The body was of four-door, four-light construction, and seated four passengers. There was no heater, nor provision for one, and the boot was reached only from inside the car by tipping forward the backrest of the rear seat. The spare wheel was exposed to the elements in a recess at the back of the body, and the twin windscreen wipers hung down rather precariously from their pivots above the windscreen. The bonnet hinged in the middle in traditional fashion, and the whole presented a neat if not particularly distinguished profile.

Yet the 170V was rather more than the little family car which its appearance implied. Most interesting, perhaps, was its backbone chassis, which was of cruciform shape and used deep oval-section tubes where many of its contemporaries were still of channel-section perimeter-frame construction. The body was supported on three tubular outriggers each side, which also served front and rear as jacking points. To this extremely rigid chassis was added not only independent front suspension – which had just been coming into vogue in the later 1930s – but also independent rear suspension, which was not common even on much more expensive cars until many years later. The front stub-axles were independently sprung by an ingenious arrangement of twin transverse leaf springs, one mounted above the other, and piston-type dampers gave control of wheel movements. At the rear, the car had Daimler-Benz's famous swing-axle arrangement first productionized in 1931, in which the drive-shafts pivoted from a fixed differential. Springing here was by means of coils, damped once again by piston-type shock absorbers.

All this gave a high level of ride comfort by the standards of

The first postwar 170V saloons were to a specification very similar to that of this prewar example, with no external access to the luggage boot.

the day, and an overall robustness which was beautifully matched by the engine and transmission. With 38bhp at full bore from its 1,697cc four-cylinder side-valve engine, the 170V could never be said to have been a great performer, but it did seem to go on forever without the need for a major overhaul. Partly, no doubt, this was due to the relatively high gearing, which meant that the engine was far from being strained when the car was flat-out at 62mph or so in top gear. Acceleration of sorts could be had by making good use of the gearbox, a tough little all-synchromesh four-speed unit (prewar 170V models had had no synchromesh on bottom gear) with a nice change action from its floor-mounted central gear-lever.

Between the 170V's introduction in 1935 and the suspension of production in 1942, 91,048 of all types had been built – huge numbers to testify to its popularity, if not also to its overall excellence. Total 170V production in 1946 was a mere 214 units, but as the passenger cars came on stream, so the numbers increased in 1947 to 1,045, and the following year to 5,116. After December 1948, pressure on Daimler-Benz's own body plant was relieved when the ambulance bodies were farmed out to the Lueg concern in Bochum, and the 1949 production figure for 170V models reached a peak of 13,101. Without a doubt, the determination of Daimler-Benz to rise from the ashes of its ruin played a large part in this success story, but equally there can be

no doubt that without the socioeconomic changes forced upon Germany by the occupying powers in the late 1940s, the company's revival would have been very much slower. By the time of the Hanover Fair which opened on May 18, 1949, Daimler-Benz were able to unveil their first all-new postwar truck (the L3500) and two new saloon cars – the 170D and 170S models.

1949: The 170D and 170S

Actually, the 170D was not really a new model at all, but simply a re-engined 170V. Its new engine, designed by Heinz Hoffmann, was a lightweight diesel unit sharing the same cylinder dimensions as the 170V's petrol engine and putting out the same 38bhp at 3,200rpm. Although pushrod-operated overhead valves replaced the petrol engine's side valves and the cylinder head featured precombustion chambers, the design of all the diesel engine's other major components was identical to those of the 170V unit. Thus great savings in tooling and manufacturing costs were made through the high degree of parts interchangeability between the 170V and 170D engines.

It should not be forgotten that the diesel-powered passenger car was still something of a novelty in 1949. The first production diesel car had been the prewar 260D Mercedes-Benz, but this had had a relatively large 2.6-litre engine, and owners had been

Although the first postwar 170-series cars were petrol-engined, a diesel version, the 170D, was introduced in 1949 with the same power output of 38bhp from the same displacement of 1,697cc.

obliged to put up with a great deal of noise and vibration as well as a lethargic performance in return for its excellent fuel economy. The adaptation of an existing petrol engine to diesel operation – and a relatively small one at that – therefore represented a major step forward. To be able to introduce it in 1949, when diesel oil in Germany was only a quarter of the price of petrol, showed far-sighted thinking at Stuttgart, for here was a four-door saloon of normal size which cost no more to run than a motorcycle.

Even though the 170D (D for Diesel) was a case of the right car at the right time, the traditional drawbacks of the compression-ignition engine had not all been eliminated. Although the mechanically-governed 170D engine had an identical power output to its petrol equivalent, and nearly the same top speed could be achieved in favourable conditions, it *was* slightly down on torque, and an overall increase in weight of around 110lb in the diesel car led to fairly leisurely acceleration. Driving characteristics were different, too, for the direct connection between accelerator and diesel injection pump meant that the throttle could not be feathered as in petrol-

engined cars. The infamous diesel 'knock' and vibration at idling speed were also present in abundance; but many customers were prepared to put up with such minor inconveniences to get a car which could regularly achieve 40mpg as against the 23mpg or so of the 170V. The 170D was available only as a four-door saloon, and was in all respects apart from its engine identical to the contemporary 170V. From 1951 its sales far outstripped those of its petrol-engined equivalent.

While the 170D introduced an economy-model Mercedes-Benz into the postwar scene, the 170S (S for Super) broadened the range upwards into a more expensive market sector, and the fact that its announcement in March 1949 was accompanied by the launch of two cabriolet derivatives demonstrated that Daimler-Benz were confident enough to enter the leisure and luxury motoring markets once more. In particular, the three 170S models were aimed at export markets, and they and the 170D were the first postwar Mercedes-Benz cars to be offered outside their native Germany.

Despite sales literature which made the model out to be a thoroughly modern piece of engineering, the 170S concept in fact dated back to around 1939. In saloon form it resembled a rather heavier 170V, and its body actually derived from that of the 1939 six-cylinder 230 model, many of the tools for which had survived the war. Experimental vehicles with 170 engines in 230 bodies had existed at the outbreak of war, and it seems that some were driven throughout the hostilities by senior Daimler-Benz employees. These, then, were effectively the 170S prototypes – although a good deal of work had also gone into the design after 1946.

The 170S was both longer and wider than the cheaper models,

the extra width giving a welcome increase in shoulder-room for passengers while the extra length resulted from a bigger boot with external access through a hinged lid. In the lower compartment of this boot was not only the spare wheel, but also just enough space for one of the ubiquitous 4½-gallon wartime jerrycans, so that the driver could carry spare fuel with him if he wished – and if he could get any! Other body changes made the 170S saloon instantly recognizable. The rear quarter-panels were heavier than on the 170V and bore witness to increased rear headroom, while the front wings reached lower at their leading

The semaphore turn indicator boxes and wind-deflectors over the front windows appeared on 1949 cars, but the opening boot-lid was not introduced until the a-suffix models arrived in 1950.

This drawing from a 1952 170V catalogue confirms that on this model the instruments were still centrally located on a rather plain dashboard, as on prewar cars, whereas by this time the 170S models had dials directly in front of the driver.

edges. The bonnet sides bore horizontal louvres picked out with chrome strips instead of the vertical slats shared by 170V and 170D models, and a chrome strip ran along the body sides and bonnet at waist level. The old folding bonnet had been replaced by one of alligator type with fixed sides (although these were demountable if necessary), and the windscreen wipers pivoted from the scuttle. Heavier bumpers were fitted, with smart chromed overriders, while the semaphore direction indicators were neatly recessed into the B/C posts, eliminating the ugly boxes fitted as afterthoughts to the 170V and 170D models.

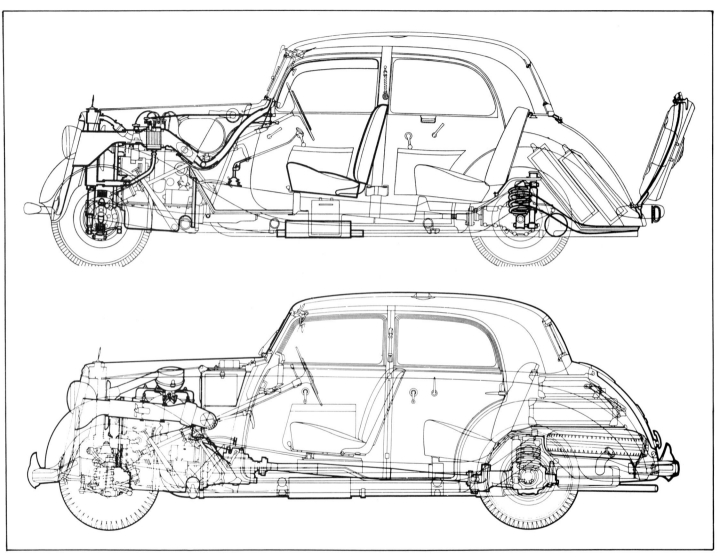

These side-elevation drawings highlight the significant differences between the 170V and 170S saloons and the much improved luggage accommodation of the latter model as a result of the extended bodywork. The wheelbase of the two cars is the same.

This high-angle view of the 1949 170S saloon emphasizes the revised front wing-line, the chromed strips on the bonnet louvres and the generally heavier appearance of the bodywork.

Comfort was ensured by soft but supportive cloth-covered seats, while the more modern dashboard presented its instruments directly ahead of the driver. If the indicators operated by the horn ring remained idiosyncratic, at least the new Mercedes-Benz had taken a decisive step or two into the modern idiom.

Improvements in appointments such as the 170S enjoyed all add weight, of course. To keep performance up to the mark, the old 170V side-valve engine had been overbored to give a cubic capacity of 1,767cc, which together with a new light-alloy head and a downdraught carburettor resulted in a 37% power increase. Better breathing had also raised the peak of the power curve by 400rpm, so tougher main and big-end bearings were specified, along with a full-flow oil filter to ensure that the higher crankshaft speeds would not affect durability. The peak of the torque curve was also higher than in the 1,697cc engine, which enabled the fitting of a lower axle ratio to compensate

further for the extra weight. Gearbox ratios remained unchanged, while vibration of the floor-change lever was minimized through rubber mountings. The extra weight of the 170S plus its bigger engine did mean a fuel consumption penalty, but customers were rewarded with better acceleration and top speed than in the cheaper models.

To match the performance improvements, there had also been chassis changes, and the 170S had wider tyres running on smaller 15in wheels, with larger brakes to ensure adequate stopping power (though pedal pressures were disturbingly high). Its front suspension had been completely redesigned to incorporate wishbones and coil springs in a layout almost identical to that of the 1937-39 Grand Prix cars. Top and bottom wishbones were mounted on a pivot which ran through the chassis frame, and about which the whole hub and suspension assembly was free to swing. Fore-and-aft movement was limited

Although it was not to reappear after the war, this picture makes it evident that the 1939 230 saloon was very much the styling forerunner of the 170S of a decade later, as well as of the 220 model which would follow it in due course.

by rubber buffers, while the coil spring sat between the wishbones and a hydraulic telescopic damper within the spring controlled wheel movements. At the rear, the swing-axle suspension had angled telescopic shock absorbers instead of the 170V's piston-type, and the rear track had been widened, although neither did anything to improve the infamous oversteering-in-the-wet tendency. Rubber mounting of both front and rear suspension did reduce noise levels, however, and the ride was considerably softer than in the older car. At the rear, the chassis frame was slightly longer to support the larger boot, and now carried the petrol tank, which had been scuttle-mounted and had held 10 fewer litres on earlier models. Rather

quaint anachronisms for a 1949 car were the 6-volt electrics and the retention of a plunger-operated chassis lubrication system, albeit with bigger-bore oilways than on previous models.

The cabriolet and coupe versions of the 170S shared the mechanical specification of the saloon exactly. Closest in appearance to the saloon was the so-called cabriolet B, which retained the four/five seat capability of the closed model, but featured only two wide doors and a convertible top. Echoing prewar German practice, this avoided impinging on boot space by folding down to a rather inelegant mass which then sat protruding backwards over the rear of the car. Its pram-irons and tiny slit rear window were also typically Teutonic in

The rolling chassis of the 170S featuring coil-spring independent suspension all round and a backbone-type tubular-steel chassis-frame. The 1,767cc engine delivered 52bhp at 4,000rpm with the modest 6.5:1 compression ratio necessary for the poor-quality fuel available at the time.

conception. Much prettier was the cabriolet A, a two-door model with what would nowadays politely be described as 2+2 seating. In fact, Daimler-Benz were so sure that the rear seat would not be sat upon that they offered a set of fitted luggage which went neatly into the compartment behind the front seats!

The cabriolet A body-style retained some of the lightness associated with the 170V and 170D models: front wings had a sweeping cutaway at their lower rear edges, and chrome was used to brighten the car's appearance – on the headlamp shells, around the windows and windscreen pillars, and in a strip below

33

The addition of the 170S to the Mercedes-Benz range was the signal for the re-introduction of a choice of open-top bodywork. This is the cabriolet A, the stowed hood of which did not look too obtrusive.

This is the cabriolet B version of the 170S, which was rated a four-five-seater and was nearly 20% cheaper than the cabriolet A, although still some 27% more expensive than the 170S saloon.

Despite the popularity of the 170S models, the 170V and 170D continued to outsell them until the earlier design was discontinued at the end of 1952. This is one of the final versions, the 170Vb.

Another view of the same car, revealing the larger bumpers and many other detail refinements which had been added to the car during its five-year postwar production run.

This rear view of a 1952 170DS saloon reveals the neater appearance achieved by mounting the boot-lid hinges internally. Earlier examples had twin chromed external hinges behind the rear window.

1950: The 170Va and 170Da

With the five-model 170 range now established, Daimler-Benz were able to turn their attention to the upper end of the market, as the later 220 and 300 ranges showed, but the 170 range was not allowed to stand still. Detail changes to the 170S during 1949 included the addition of chromed dashboard knobs and a two-tone horn, while the optional heater was standardized and a better spare wheel fixing was introduced. 1950's news was wider rear tracks for the V and D models, which from June 1950 were redesignated 170Va and 170Da, respectively, when a series of improvements arrived. The a-suffix cars were never identifiable as such by badging, but they could be recognized by their hinged boot-lids. As there was no change to the boot itself, however, the spare wheel remained exposed on the outside of the new lid. Transparent wind-deflectors were also fitted to the front windows. More important, though, was the fitting to both models of 1,767cc engines, the 170Va getting a slightly detuned 170S unit with an updraught carburettor and 45bhp, while the

The dashboard of a 1952 170DS with a large clock matching the speedometer. Note that the gear-lever has been moved from the floor to the steering column.

the running-boards, as well as for a waist strip which terminated neatly above the rear wing. Plain bonnet sides contributed to the streamlined look, and the car had separate sidelights for the first time, mounted in chromed housings on the crown of the front wings.

At over one and a half times the price of the 170S saloon, even in Germany, the cabriolet A did not find many buyers, and like the cabriolet B it was withdrawn at the end of 1951 (some sources say earlier) when the saloon still had several years of production ahead of it. During that final year of production, many potential buyers had doubtless defected to the visually similar but much more rapid 220 cabriolet, with its six-cylinder engine, for the open cars really appealed to the driver whose desire for something a little different was greater than his need to watch his bank balance.

170Da engine shared the enlarged 75mm bore of the petrol unit to give only 2bhp extra, but at a higher crankshaft speed of 5,200rpm. Both models also had telescopic shock absorbers and the larger brakes of the 170S.

Modifications made during the autumn of 1950 included reclining front seats with detachable headrests (commonly supplied for the passenger seat only). These became optional on the two cheaper models and standard on the 170S saloons and cabriolets, and all models could be bought with a Becker radio. For the three 170S models, it was possible to order a hinged fitting allowing a second spare wheel to be carried externally at the rear. Windscreens were supplied after September by Sigla instead of Sekurit, and the open cars were sensibly provided with lockable glove boxes. January 1951 saw the arrival of a sliding steel sunroof as standard on the two petrol-engined saloons, a fitment which the 170Da would not get for some six months. The rest of 1951 witnessed only the loss of the two 170S cabriolet models, the deletion from the 170S of the hand-throttle control which improving petrol quality had rendered almost superfluous, and the arrival on the same model of an optional heater blower.

1952: The 170DS and 170Sb, 170Vb and 170Db
The great popularity of the diesel models made it inevitable that Stuttgart should 'dieselize' the up-market 170S as a companion to the 170D, and this they did in February 1952 when the 170DS appeared. At the same time, the existing 170S became a 170Sb in name, if not in badging, and the 170V and D models – still bearing an a-suffix – were given hypoid rear axles. For reasons best known to Stuttgart's engineers, the new 170DS and 170Sb models came under the works designation W191, when all the other 170 variants had shared the W136 designation, but that designation implied nothing more than a slightly wider rear track than on the superseded 170S and a rather nasty column gear-change, both inherited from the six-cylinder 220 model. Both cars were heavier than the old 170S, the 170Sb compensating through a lower axle ratio, while the 170DS retained the high ratio of the other diesel models, but coupled to a slight increase in torque. Visually, the two models were indistinguishable unless sharp eyes spotted the larger 16in and narrower 5.50 tyres of the diesel-engined car, and of course there were identifying badges on the boot-lids.

In May 1952, the 170Va and 170Da became the 170Vb and 170Db, respectively, as they, like the S models, gained wider rear tracks. Recognition features came in the shape of the heavier S-type bumpers and the horizontal louvres – again of S-type derivation – in the bonnet sides, which nevertheless remained of the old folding pattern. The 170DS and Sb

The final fling for the 170 range was to offer 170S-V and 170S-D versions, which were essentially S-type bodies mounted on the cheaper V and D chassis, respectively.

remained in production until August 1953, and the 170Vb and 170Db until September and October of that year, respectively, the only notable changes in the meantime being padded sun visors for the cheaper models in June 1952, and a revised instrument panel on the Sb after July the following year.

1953: The 170S-V and 170S-D
If it had seemed like a good idea at the time to match the 170V and 170D models with corresponding up-market versions in the 170S and 170DS, the actual effect of all this model diversification had simply been to spread customer allegiance across a wider range rather than to increase overall sales of the 170 series. As radically new replacement models were also on the horizon, it made sense for Daimler-Benz to slim down the 170 range for its final years, and this they did in the 170S-V and 170S-D models.

These two new models completely replaced the four earlier 170 types from July 1953, although stocks of the old models lingered on until well into 1954. Stuttgart's intention had been to combine the equipment levels of the old S models with the economy and cheapness of the 170V and 170D – and indeed the 170S-V was cheaper to buy than the 170S, and the 170S-D cheaper than the superseded 170DS. In all honesty, the 170S-D

was scarcely changed from its predecessor, the only differences lying in a modified fuel injection system, the 14.1:1 steering ratio, and the leaf-spring front suspension inherited from the 170D. The 170S-V was a similar hybrid, with the 170V engine, steering, leaf-spring front suspension (though admittedly somewhat softened) and the high axle ratio which the diesel model had already, all fitted to the 170S body. Recognition features of the 170S-V and S-D models were the absence of chrome trim on the bonnet louvres and of bumper overriders. Doubtless with the same aim of minimizing costs, the sliding steel sunroof could no longer be had, although a cheaper full-length fabric sunroof was made available for both models. Eight body colours and various interior materials brightened the range up a little, but sadly both models retained column gear-changes.

Neither of these models really added to the reputation of the 170 series. Their handling and performance were inferior to those of the real S-type 170 models, and this retrograde step at a time when the 170 series was beginnning to look very dated indeed cannot have done much for the Daimler-Benz sales figures. The petrol-engined version sold a miserable 3,122 examples in three seasons, although its thunder was admittedly stolen by the new 180 model; but the 170S-D sold strongly despite the availability of the new 180D. There were no changes

The 220 saloon, which was introduced in 1951, marked the appearance of a 2,195cc six-cylinder engine developing 80bhp. Although based on the 170S body, the car was immediately identifiable from its four-cylinder counterpart by the headlamps, which had been faired into the reprofiled front wings, as well as by the additional use of chrome.

Like the 170S, the 220 saloon was to be augmented by more sporting body styles. This is the 1953 cabriolet A, a two-three-seater, the wing-line of which, perhaps, could not quite match the grace of the 170S equivalent.

of consequence during the models' lifetime, with the exception of a boot division introduced in January 1954. Production of the 170S-V stopped in February 1955, while that of the 170S-D continued until September that year.

The 220

Before the Hitler War, the little 170V had been matched by the six-cylinder 230 model of generally similar proportions, and from which the 170S had later been developed. A six-cylinder complement to the 170V was also planned postwar, and at the Frankfurt Motor Show of April 1951 – when the 170Va, Da, S saloon and S cabriolets were already flying the Mercedes-Benz flag high – the new 220 model was introduced.

As ever, Fritz Nallinger's engineers had made intelligent and economical use of the resources available to them. The 220 was actually not much more than a 170S body and chassis with a highly efficient new six-cylinder 2,195cc power unit installed. Yet the fact that it had six cylinders, and that the basic saloon was accompanied by cabriolet A and cabriolet B models in exactly the same way as the original 170S, contributed to precisely that aura of one-upmanship which was what Nallinger wanted. If the 170S was aimed at the well-to-do middle-classes, then the 220 was aimed at the professional man.

Stuttgart had done a good job of concealing the fact that the 220 and the 170S shared the same body. The main recognition feature was that the 220's headlamps were faired into the leading edges of the front wings, and that the crowns of these wings were surmounted by chrome strakes to give a streamlined effect. It

was simple, but it worked. Inside, things were also much the same as for 170S models, with the same dashboard bedecked with additional chrome fittings; but there was still utilitarian rubber flooring at the front instead of carpeting. Upholstery was cloth-covered as standard, and loose seat covers were optionally available. In traditional Mercedes-Benz style, everything about the car was solid – and heavy. At 2,970lb, the 220 weighed-in about 110lb heavier than the heaviest of the 170 models.

The car was intended as a rapid autobahn-cruiser, which meant that its engine had to stand up to prolonged full-throttle work. To this end, its designers had aimed at a relatively high rpm limit without loss of the traditional Mercedes-Benz reliability or robustness. The higher crankshaft speeds were achieved mainly through better breathing, promoted by large valves operated by a chain-driven overhead camshaft. To give adequate space for the valves, the combustion chambers in the cylinder head extended beyond the confines of the cylinder bores, and the valves themselves were not directly in line, but staggered. At 4,850rpm, 80bhp was available, which at 36bhp per litre represented a far greater specific output than that of the

contemporary 170V petrol engine, drawn up in an age when engine longevity was achieved principally through understressed, low-revving designs.

Short strokes are better suited than long ones to the greater stresses of a high-revving engine, so the 220 unit was of over-square design (80×72.88mm), which brought with it a shallow, sturdy cylinder block and a strong crankshaft. To ensure smooth running at high speeds, a vibration damper was fitted to the front of the crankshaft, while inserts for the exhaust valves in the chrome nickel iron cylinder head guarded against possible durability problems. The water jacket extended right down to the crankshaft centreline for optimum cooling of the bores, and incorporated an oil cooler – partly because the designers wanted to take no risks over the use of the newly-available thinner oils. The blocks were cast with open sides for ease of inspection on assembly, and closed up with bolted plates.

Wheels and tyres were the same as on the 170S, but there were changes to the overall gearing. A lower ratio in the hypoid-bevel final drive improved acceleration in the upper ratios, but first and second speeds in the all-synchromesh gearbox were raised to maintain low-speed docility. Gear-changing was effected for the first time on a Mercedes-Benz by a currently-fashionable column-mounted lever, a concession to American taste which most contemporary road-testers felt it polite not to discuss. Brakes were unchanged from the 170S, although heavy pedal pressures made them distinctly worrying if used at the car's 90mph top speed. An anti-roll bar at the front ensured that enthusiastic drivers would not get themselves into difficulties. The extra pair of cylinders and the extra performance, of course, incurred a fuel consumption penalty, but the 19mpg overall figure was somewhat offset by a fuel tank containing nearly 5 gallons more than that of the 170S, thus enabling long drives between refuelling stops to be made. Curiously, though, the anachronistic 6-volt electrical system was retained.

Although the 220 enjoyed steady sales, it was never exactly a runaway success. Sales peaked at 9,165 in 1952, the second year of production, and for 1953 sales were back down to 3,322, while the following and final year they were laughably small at 214 cars. Export sales were limited; the car was not imported into North America, and at £2,022 14s 2d (including a massive £595 14s 2d Purchase Tax) in the UK in 1954, it was ridiculously expensive and made few friends despite its unquestionable virtues.

Nevertheless, some eight times as many 220 saloons were made as the equivalent cabriolet and coupe models. Prices no doubt restrained the sales of these more prestigious variants, the four-seater cabriolet B costing nearly 40% more in Germany than the equivalent saloon, the cabriolet A having a huge 70% price increment, and the coupe when it arrived being even more expensive than that. The open 220 models nevertheless remained in production some 15 months after the last saloon had been made, and indeed the coupe's introduction was delayed until saloon assembly stopped in May 1954.

Like the saloon, the two-door 220 models were really hybrids, with the six-cylinder engine in 170S bodies, but again they were instantly recognizable by the headlamps sunk into the wings. As flashing indicators had superseded the semaphore type of the 170S models, front flashers were incorporated in the chrome trim on the wing crowns, and were matched at the rear by indicator lights in chromed pods mounted on the curved panel just above the rear wings. The cabriolet A and coupe models –

Added to the 220 range in 1954, the coupe was based on the cabriolet A design and was equipped with a sliding steel sunroof. This is by far the rarest of the 220 range, only 85 examples having been produced.

which were simply cabriolet A bodies with a fixed roof and a sliding steel sunroof as standard – were also distinguished by a polished stone-guard at the leading edge of the rear wings, while twin driving lamps were a standard fitting. Mechanically, the three special-bodied models were identical to the saloon, the cabriolet B nonetheless losing less than 1mph from its top speed, despite a weight some 170lb greater than the saloon's, and the cabriolet A actually being about 3mph faster, despite carrying the same increased weight. In all cases, the increased weight incurred a minor fuel consumption penalty.

Production of the 220 saloons ended in May 1954, two months after pilot production of the replacement 220a Ponton model had begun at Stuttgart. The cabriolets and coupes were directly replaced after August the following year by equivalent Ponton models with full-width bodywork.

Police, light commercial and other special variants of the 170 and 220

Postwar production of 170V models had begun with pick-up

41

trucks, vans and ambulances, all with very spartan and boxy bodywork. The lines of the Sindelfingen ambulance body became softer for 1948 models, but the utility lines of the vans and pick-ups remained a year longer. Sindelfingen continued building vans on the 170V and 170D chassis until the b-suffix variants ceased production in 1953, but after 1948, construction of the ambulance bodies was farmed out to Lueg, in Bochum, who had built a total of 1,070 by the end of 170Vb/Db production. The original four-window version had been replaced by a six-window model when the a-suffix chassis went into production, and a twin-stretcher body was made available when the b-suffix models were announced.

For 1953, the basic Lueg body style was offered in three versions, the ambulance being supplemented by a 5/7-seater kombi, or estate car, and by a service van in which the rearmost windows were replaced by panels to form a van back, while four doors and five seats remained available. These variants, introduced on the 170Vb/Db and 170S, could be had until 1955, and it seems likely that the very last 'new' 170 models for sale would have been 170S-V or S-D chassis with ambulance, van, or kombi bodies built at Bochum.

Lueg also introduced a special six-seater taxi body in 1949 on the 170V and 170D chassis. Intended for export only, this had a higher roofline than the standard saloon, while the rear of the body was vertical, with no protruding boot. The rear seat was repositioned over the axle, and rearward-facing seats were installed at the front of the rear compartment. These taxis, most popular on diesel-engined chassis for obvious reasons, seem to have been available until the end of 170S-D/S-V production. They were a familiar sight on the streets of Copenhagen for many years.

Special police models were also built on the 170 and 220 chassis. Initially, the police made do with 170V pick-ups adapted as personnel-carriers with inward-facing slatted seats for six in the pick-up bed and a canvas tilt. However, Sindelfingen introduced a special, rather crude, four-door cabriolet-type body on the 170Da chassis, with a rough-and-ready convertible top and detachable sidescreens instead of wind-up windows. Cars fitted with this – also sold on the 170Db chassis, but still with the louvred bonnet of the a-suffix cars – were known as OTP models (Offener Tourenwagen für Polizei, or police open tourer), and all were basically similar and shared

This was the Sindelfingen factory's own van bodywork as fitted to the 170D chassis between 1951 and 1953. Like the passenger car models, it followed very closely the company's prewar design.

Lueg's characteristic ambulance body was adapted to four instead of the usual six side windows to provide a four-five-door Mercedes-Benz service vehicle. The chassis is either a 170Vb or a 170Db, dating from 1952-53.

43

A 170S Police model, kitted out as an eight-seater personnel carrier. When erected, the hood covered both compartments and incorporated twin side windows as well as a large window above the rear door for the benefit of the sideways-facing occupants.

the mechanical specification of the equivalent saloon. Most wore the distinctive green livery of the German police, but some saw service as military staff cars. The police forces of Trier and Hanover took similar bodies on 220 chassis, but only 41 of this variant were made in all. In addition, a few eight-seater open bodies with truck-like rear quarters were built by Binz on 170S chassis, and 170S, Sb, S-D and 220 models with uprated electrical equipment and kombi- or taxi-type bodies by Binz and Lueg, respectively, were available to police forces as radio patrol cars.

Finally, mention should be made of a pair of special two-door cabriolets built in 1962 by German coachbuilders, which claimed two of only 47 bare 220 chassis to escape from Stuttgart. Built by Drews, in Essen, and Wendler, in Reutlingen, both were early attempts at full-width styling and were probably inspired by the shape of the 300SL racers. Neither, however, was an aesthetic success, and both remained one-offs.

The 170 and 220 models in Great Britain and the USA
The 170 models are looked upon today with considerable nostalgic affection in West Germany and other European countries where their sales were numerous, but in Great Britain and the USA they always remained rarities. Only tiny numbers of postwar Mercedes-Benz cars had made their way to the United States before 1952, when Stuttgart signed an agreement with the Hoffmann Motor Company, of New York, for national distribution of Mercedes-Benz cars in the USA. Even then, sales figures remained minuscule: only 36 vehicles passed through Hoffmann's hands in the first 12 months of their distributorship, and it would be true to say that when significantly better sales figures were achieved it was due to the impact of the sporting 300SL and 190SL models rather than to the staid old 170 and 220 saloons, which by American standards of the early 1950s were terribly outdated designs. Nevertheless, a few enthusiastic buyers were found for the cabriolet and coupe models.

As for Britain, foreign car imports were only a trickle until the relaxation of import restrictions in 1954, and Mercedes-Benz were unable to gain a foothold before that date. The leading motoring magazines had kept readers abreast of developments through reports of road tests on the cars conducted abroad, but Import and Purchase Taxes ensured that the cars found few customers when they did become readily available in Great Britain. After 1954, a few 220 saloons were sold, but cabriolet and coupe versions remained very rare indeed.

CHAPTER 3

Prestige restored

The 300 and 300S models

Before the Second World War, the flagship of the Mercedes-Benz range had been a large, rapid, luxury touring car, and so it was that the arrival at the September 1951 Frankfurt Show of the 300 models represented not only a significant technical achievement, but also an important milestone in the rebuilding of the Daimler-Benz company. It is said that chief engineer Fritz Nallinger concentrated on the 300's development to the virtual exclusion of all else, so important was the car for company – and no doubt Nallinger's own – morale during a difficult period.

By 1951, there were signs that the expensive luxury car was re-emerging in Germany as the 'economic miracle' got under way, although there could be no doubt that a car such as the 300 would have to rely fairly heavily on export sales. Daimler-Benz had their eyes firmly set on the North American market, which was not only much larger, but also in a much healthier state than any of the European markets, and so it was not surprising that the 300 showed American influence in a number of areas. Yet Stuttgart's designers clearly felt that a good measure of traditionalism was called for in a large, formal, luxury saloon such as the 300 was meant to be, and so the column gear-change and the abundance of chrome which grew greater with succeeding versions were combined with a very conservatively styled body. This was to be a car for rich businessmen and Heads of State, and indeed it was adopted by the Federal German Government as their official car during the 1950s. So closely identified did the 300 become with the leading political figures of that era that it is still often referred to as the 'Adenauer car'.

The 300

The chassis of the 300 was of the familiar Mercedes-Benz type, with deep oval tubes forming an X-shaped backbone frame, and tubular outriggers on which the body was mounted. In Frankfurt Show form, it exactly paralleled the 170S type with rear-mounted petrol tank, but by the time full-scale production of the 300 began in November 1951, further testing of the pilot-build cars had shown up a need for greater torsional stiffness, and the production vehicles had reinforcing plates welded to the tube in the centre of the frame. Suspension brought no major surprises, although the wishbone-and-coil-spring IFS was bolstered by an anti-roll bar, and the coil-sprung swing-axles at the rear benefited from an ingenious ride-selection arrangement. In this, activation of a facia-mounted switch caused an electric servo motor to engage a pair of auxiliary torsion bars. These had the effect of stiffening the rear suspension by some 33%, which meant that good handling qualities could be maintained when the car was heavily laden, while at the same time soft springing could be used to give a luxury-car ride under normal conditions.

The first season's 300 models had worm steering, which paralleled that of the 170 and 220 models but was slightly lower-geared, but for the 1953 season a recirculating-ball system was introduced, which was both lower-geared and more accurate. The unassisted hydraulic drum brakes represented a weakness, however, being somewhat marginal for a car of the 300's weight and requiring high pedal pressures in the best Mercedes-Benz fashion. The final drive was of the new hypoid-bevel type, as introduced simultaneously on the 220, but the centralized

An early 300 saloon, dating from 1951. The W186 models were the first Mercedes-Benz cars to have the larger star motif on the wheel trims.

A high-angle view of the 300 chassis showing clearly the cruciform tubular construction. The six-cylinder 2,996cc engine was rated at 115bhp at 4,600rpm for its first three years of production.

chassis lubrication system was an anachronism which showed that Daimler-Benz had yet to get to grips with the latest sealed-bearing technology, even if a facia warning light which reminded the driver every hundred miles to pump the plunger at his feet was a sophisticated advance. At least the 12-volt electrics showed a willingness to accept modern automotive practice.

A good deal of interest centred on the 2,996cc six-cylinder engine, which shared the 220 engine's philosophy of a short stroke to permit high operating speeds. In execution, it differed greatly from the smaller 'six', however, being slightly under-square and sharing only its overhead camshaft and staggered valve arrangement with the 220 unit. Its general layout was fairly conventional, with a cast-iron block, light-alloy head and chain-driven camshaft, but particularly notable was the use of a sloping-head arrangement in which the joint face between the block and cylinder head was angled at 30 degrees. This permitted even larger diameter valves, which contributed to the

The type 300's independent rear suspension. The electric servo motor which brings the auxiliary torsion bars into operation is visible in the foreground.

The coil-spring independent front suspension of a 1951 type 300, meticulous preparation having gone into this display chassis.

good breathing so necessary in an engine designed for high-speed use. Shaped piston crowns gave a wedge-shaped combustion chamber, into which the spark plugs protruded through holes in the cylinder block. A seven-bearing crankshaft promised long running life as well as smooth operation, and indeed Daimler-Benz were at pains to point out that a properly-maintained 300 engine should need no major overhaul work for at least 60,000 and possibly 100,000 miles.

The automatic choke fitted to the twin Solex dual downdraught carburettors was both an advanced feature as European cars went and a reminder of the American influence on the design of the 300. Yet in spite of the 115bhp on tap, it took a long stretch of road to wind this 3,900lb motor car up to the 100mph maximum of which it was just capable. Consistent with the usual Mercedes-Benz high gearing, not a lot of acceleration was available in top gear, but 80 or 90mph could be maintained more or less indefinitely without strain on either the mechanical components or the passengers, and an overall fuel

The 2,996cc OHV engine of the 300 saloon in 1951 form, with twin Solex 40 PBJC downdraught carburettors and a power output of 115bhp at 4,600rpm.

consumption of around 17mpg was good for a powerful and heavy 3-litre luxury saloon in the early 1950s. Rapid acceleration was available, of course, if the driver made judicious use of the all-synchromesh gearbox, which contained ratios unique to the 300 and was rather nicer to use than the column change might have led one to expect; but the penalties were increased fuel consumption and excessive tyre wear, which was already rapid enough on these heavy cars.

The interior was a curious mixture of the traditional and what Germans euphemistically call the baroque. The facia, for example, was surmounted by a polished wood fillet, but the combined instrument gauge was in garish Transatlantic style, and a thick chrome strip running right across the lower edge of the facia only contributed to the general aesthetic disaster. Nevertheless, the first-class build quality almost excused such shortcomings, and the two-spoke steering wheel with its chromed horn ring, which replaced the traditional Mercedes-Benz three-spoke type, certainly was an improvement. The deep, comfortable seats were covered in cloth as standard, but leather was available and was probably more common in

The bumper overriders and the perforated wheel trims distinguish this 1954 300b saloon from earlier 300 models. This is a right-hand-drive example registered in the UK.

48

Rear view of the car pictured on the previous page and below. Luggage accommodation was on a scale befitting a car of this size and quality, and there was even space for two spare wheels if necessary.

A look inside the 300b to see how the front passenger's seat could be lowered to form a temporary bed with the rear seat cushion. Note the swivelling pane of the rear door window. Like most Mercedes-Benz cars imported into the UK at the time, this example has leather upholstery.

markets like the UK, where wood and leather were still expected in a luxury car. Fully-reclining front seats were standard, and a detachable passenger headrest was available. Some cars were built with a division between front and rear compartments. Unexpected items were the full-length grab rails above the doors and – well in advance of its time – a steering lock operated by the ignition key.

One of the essentials of a large luxury car is plenty of room for its occupants, and the 300 excelled in this department. Sitting on a 120-inch wheelbase, it also looked the part, and the styling emphasized the overall impression of size. Photographs of prototypes show the car conceived initially as a stretched 170S/220, but the arrival of a sweeping front wing line impinging on the doors and of a much reworked cabin area lent the car the

necessary air of distinction. Headlights on the production cars were recessed into the wings, 220-fashion, while chrome strips on the front wing crowns like those of the 220 cabriolet terminated in indicator lights, and twin foglamps were standard. The rear indicators unfortunately came in chromed pods, surely an afterthought to the neat rear light clusters, which included reversing lights. Doors were all hinged at their leading edges, thus breaking with the 170/220 tradition, and the trailing edges of the side windows bore hinged vent panes inside the main glasses, which were designed to deflect draughts when the windows were open. As for the boot, that was every bit as big as the 300's customers could have wished for, with room for *two* spare wheels if required in addition to a veritable mountain of luggage. Characteristically, Daimler-Benz offered a set of fitted

Built on a shorter-wheelbase version of
the 300 chassis and powered by a 150bhp,
triple-carburettor variant of the 2,996cc
engine, the 300S was offered from 1952 in
three basically similar body styles. This is
the roadster, with almost completely
disappearing hood.

The cabriolet version of the 300S is
instantly recognizable by its hood's
landau-irons, which meant that when
folded the top rested on the rear deck of
the body.

suitcases as an optional extra.

The 300 cabriolet D

It was a Mercedes-Benz tradition that the top-of-the-range car should be not a limousine, but a big open car, and when the 300 saloon was announced at the Frankfurt Show it was accompanied by the magnificent and rather more costly cabriolet D. A massive padded hood with chrome landau irons distinguished this four-door tourer from its saloon counterpart, and this hood, together with a certain amount of body reinforcement, made the cars even heavier than the saloons, to which they were in other respects identical. Intended from the outset for an exclusive clientele, the cabriolet D was hand-built in limited numbers at the Sindelfingen body works, production beginning rather later than that of the saloons in March 1952. Nevertheless, even this was not exclusive enough for some clients, and Daimler-Benz were obliged to turn out some special open 'processional' versions for Heads of State and other potentates.

The 300b

The 300b models introduced in March 1954 were designed to meet some of the criticisms which had been levelled at the original 300. An extra 10bhp had been extracted from the engine by the use of improved Solex carburettors and a higher compression ratio, which rendered the facia-mounted octane selector even more necessary than it had been on the early 300, as petrol quality was still very variable in some countries in the mid-1950s. Maximum speed was up slightly to 102mph, but more important was the improved flexibility of the engine, achieved through a massive torque increase (from 114lb/ft at 2,500rpm to 163lb/ft at 2,600rpm) and a wider spread of usable torque. Lower gearbox and axle ratios made the 300b altogether much more accelerative – indeed, almost indecently quick for such a big car – while wider brake drums with vacuum-servo assistance provided the extra stopping power to compensate.

Although the 300b's appearance was basically unchanged from that of its predecessor, a number of minor alterations made it instantly recognizable. More chrome had been loaded on in

The hood of this 300S cabriolet offers a snug fit, but the age of the adequately sized rear window had yet to arrive and rearward vision was considerably restricted.

Swivelling front quarter-lights help to identify this as a 1955 300c saloon, which was introduced towards the end of the year and used the higher-compression 125bhp version of the 2,996cc engine first seen the previous year on the 300b saloon.

the shape of bumper overriders and full-size wheel trims with perforated outer edges, and a polished stone-guard now adorned the leading edge of the rear wing. In place of the wind deflectors fitted to the front doors were swivelling quarter-lights, which inevitably brought with them more bright trim, and larger front indicator lamp units accompanied rather clumsier looking trims on the wing crowns. In all these changes, the cabriolet D models followed their saloon counterparts and, like the saloons, were slightly more expensive than their predecessors.

The 300c

The mid-1950s saw changes taking place in the market for expensive luxury cars. Under the impact of American developments, European manufacturers were being forced to introduce automatic transmission options for their most expensive vehicles, and so the 300b became a 300c in September 1955 with the option of a Borg-Warner three-speed automatic gearbox alongside the standard four-speed manual. This was characteristic of early automatic transmissions in that it did nothing for either performance or fuel consumption, but it did

lend that extra air of luxury to the proceedings and seems to have been a popular option.

A persistent complaint from enthusiastic drivers of earlier 300s (as indeed of all Mercedes-Benz products with the double-pivot swing-axle suspension) was the car's tendency to lurch into sudden oversteer in high-speed cornering – a characteristic which could be particularly disconcerting in the wet. While insisting publicly that swing-axles gave the best possible ride/handling compromise, Daimler-Benz were clearly worried about this, and the 300c was fitted with a development of the system which had only a single, low-mounted pivot. Although this version of the swing-axle suspension did not eliminate the oversteer tendency on the 300, or indeed on any other Mercedes-Benz model to which it was applied, it did alleviate the problem a little, and in conjunction with fatter tyres on the 300c it gave drivers rather more confidence in the car's handling.

In appearance, the 300c was again little changed from its predecessors, although the wider rear window and swivelling front quarter-lights were instant recognition points. Options

included a sliding steel sunroof, imitation wire wheels made by Lenmerz (which were popular in the USA) and – years before its time yet again – central locking of all the doors.

The 300 was, of course, a natural choice as a chauffeur-driven vehicle, and had been since its inception, but in the mid-1950s Daimler-Benz decided to give it an additional fillip in this market. The low-volume cabriolet D was therefore taken out of series production in June 1956 (although it is said that individual cars continued to be built to special order at Sindelfingen until the following spring), and the resources formerly devoted to its assembly were switched to a new long-wheelbase version of the closed 300. With an extra 4in in its wheelbase, this vehicle offered massive rear legroom, which was often put to good use through the installation of a division and jump-seats, which could be specified at the time of ordering. Despite being rather heavier than the standard 300, the long-wheelbase car did not lose out too much on performance, and its sales figures proved that Daimler-Benz's move had been a wise one.

54

Considerable body restyling took place in the transition from 300c to 300d saloon, the changes being most noticeable at the rear with an extended wing and boot-line and a reprofiled roof incorporating a wraparound rear window. At the front, cowls over the headlamps blended into the wings.

The 300d

If the 300 had borne distinctly conservative styling at its launch in 1951, by the mid-1950s that styling was beginning to look positively antiquated, and Daimler-Benz decided that only a major revamp of the car's appearance would keep sales at acceptable levels. Therefore, starting with the 124in wheelbase chassis, they squared up the rear end to give an even larger boot and a new wingline into which vertical tail-light clusters were incorporated, squared up the front wings to match and set sidelights below the headlights, fitted bumpers of a new shape, and redesigned the rear of the passenger cabin with a panoramic wraparound window. Interesting new features were door windows which wound down out of sight and rear side windows which could be lifted out. As the wind deflectors of previous 300 models had disappeared and a pillarless design was used, this left what was effectively an open car with a roof – a splendidly luxurious feature which would not have been possible without the great rigidity already inherent in the 300's body. After the

American hardtop vogue, which had doubtless inspired the design, Daimler-Benz referred to the 300d as a 'hardtop-limousine', when it was launched in July 1957.

Inside, things remained much as before, with deep luxurious seats in velvet, cord, or leather upholstery. The full-length grab handles in the roof were replaced by shorter handles front and rear, however, and the optional division now had an electrically-controlled glass partition, which could sink out of sight for occasions when the car was used in its 'windowless' form. After September 1958, it was possible to specify an air-conditioning unit, which was installed in the cavernous boot. As a complementary model, the sumptuous 300d cabriolet was made available in July 1958, but this was really only for State occasions, and it is doubtful whether many private buyers felt the need to reach so deeply into their pockets.

The popularity of the automatic gearbox option on the 300c had led Daimler-Benz to think about keeping the performance figures up to scratch by uprating the engine, so the standard three-speed automatic transmission in the 300d (manual was only available to special order) was coupled to a much uprated power unit with electronic fuel injection, based on the 300SL unit, but with conventional lubrication rather than a dry sump and a more conservative power output. Nevertheless, the 160bhp now available at 5,300rpm gave the 300d a considerably better performance than the Borg-Warner-equipped 300c, and a useful torque increase to 175lb/ft at 4,200rpm gave improved top-gear acceleration, which had always been one of the 300's weakest suits.

The 300d lasted in production until March 1962, when the considerably smaller W112 300SE introduced the previous year had to take its place until the massive 600 arrived in 1963. 1959-season cars had benefited from a number of changes to the control layout: deformable plastic knobs on the facia and a padded steering wheel boss as part of Stuttgart's new safety programme, a headlamp flasher switch, a smaller brake pedal, and a repositioned gear-change indicator panel on the facia; but

there were no more changes of significance. The last of the 65 cabriolets left Sindelfingen in February 1962, and the separate-chassis Mercedes-Benz passed into history.

The 300S
The 300S is perhaps best characterized by the fact that for nearly six years it was Germany's most expensive production car, and its owners tended to be international celebrities like Bing Crosby and Gary Cooper, or Heads of State like the Aga Khan, the King of Jordan, or the Shah of Iran, who wanted a personal car which matched their formal limousines in quality. The intention of the model's designers was that it should pick up where the fabulous 540K supercharged sports models had left off – and so it did, although in terms of pure performance it was outranked by the 300SL gullwing coupe, which actually sold for rather less. Such an exclusive machine inevitably sold in small numbers, and only 560 examples of the 300S were built in three years of production, while only 200 of the later 300Sc were made

With the door windows wound down out of sight and the rear side windows removed the 300d is seen to be of pillarless construction and was referred to at the time as a hardtop-saloon. Fuel injection had helped to boost its engine's output to 160bhp.

The elegant and sumptious interior of the 300d saloon, which set a standard in 1957 which few other car manufacturers could match.

in the subsequent two and a half years.

The Paris Motor Show in spring 1951 was chosen for the introduction of the 300S, although only two cars were to be built that year and production did not get under way until July 1952. The W188, as it was known within the factory, was based on a shortened version of the 300 saloon's chassis, with a 114.2in wheelbase. Suspension was unchanged from the saloon, but the brakes had finned drums for better cooling and could be provided after the end of the 1953 season with a vacuum servo at extra cost. The four-speed all-synchromesh gearbox used different ratios to those in the saloons (and later cars had another unique set of higher ratios), while the 4.125 axle made the overall gearing rather higher than the saloon's. The cars were marginally lighter than their saloon contemporaries, but the achievement of the significantly higher 110mph top speed and faster acceleration was due principally to a more powerful version of the 3-litre engine with a higher compression ratio,

triple instead of twin downdraught carburettors, and a maximum power output of 150bhp. To go with this more sporting performance, the 300S had a rather quicker recirculating-ball steering system (which was also fitted to saloon models from March 1954) and, surprisingly, thinner tyres. Its design aim as a long-distance cruiser was emphasized by the fuel tank, which held an additional 3 gallons, giving it an extra 50 to 60 miles range.

There were three versions of the 300S, although their catalogue descriptions as roadster, cabriolet A and coupe perhaps made more of the body differences than was really warranted. All shared the same 2 + 2 styling, with a body some 10in shorter overall than the 300 saloon, around 1in wider and 3½in lower. The frontal appearance was identical, but the wings swept downwards earlier along the imposing bonnet, and from there backwards the panels were all different, with the styling generally resembling the contemporary 170S and 220

This is Pininfarina's not entirely successful attempt to rebody a 1955 300S – an unhappy blend of the modern and the traditional.

Another special body by Pininfarina, this time based on a 300b chassis, although not seen in this form until 1956, by which time the 300c was in production. The straight-through wing-line has been applied much more successfully this time.

This Pininfarina body on a 1955 300S chassis was commissioned by a customer who presumably had been inspired by American styling of the late 1930s.

cabriolet A models. The boot, of course, was enormous, while the back of the token rear seat was designed to fold flat to leave additional luggage space. As usual, dealers could supply sets of fitted suitcases to fill the boot and the rear luggage area if required.

Of the three models, the coupe was the most popular and the roadster the least. All shared identical bodywork up to the waistline and had identical windscreens, but the roadster had a fully-disappearing hood without landau irons, while the cabriolet A had the traditional German heavy hood with massive chromed landau irons which when folded sat on the rear deck. The coupe was simply a roadster with a permanently fixed hardtop – and indeed a detachable hardtop was made available for the roadster which exactly resembled the coupe roof. Contrary to what its name suggested, the roadster shared winding door windows with the other two models.

All this elegant, exclusive and beautifully-finished car did not come cheaply. In Germany, a 300S cost 34,500 Deutschmarks,

compared to 22,000 Deutschmarks for a 300 saloon, and once UK Purchase Tax, import duties and so on had been added, the British price in early 1955 was around £5,530 as against the saloon's £3,300 10s 10d. When these prices are compared with the £3,385 asked for a Rolls-Royce Silver Cloud in April 1955, it is not surprising that very few 300S models went to UK buyers.

The 300Sc

Despite the dramatic decline in 300S sales which the 1954 arrival of the exciting 300SL brought about, Daimler-Benz considered it worthwhile to introduce a revised 300S range for 1956. The 300Sc thus became available from September 1955 with the fuel-injected, dry-sump, 3-litre engine from the 300SL and a number of additional modifications which increased its weight by 44lb.

The 300Sc engine was in a softer state of tune than as installed in the gullwing, putting out 175bhp at 5,400rpm as against the

The 300Sc in roadster form, which differed from the 300S in having single-pivot swing-axle rear suspension and a fuel-injected 175bhp version of the 2,996cc engine.

215bhp at 5,800rpm of the full-blooded 300SL production engine. Top speed was only 2mph up on the 300S at 112mph, but the real improvement came in the astonishing flexibility offered by the fuel-injected engine. Gear ratios were changed again, with a lower third to boost acceleration, but higher first and second speeds, all matched to the original axle ratio. In the mid-1950s, an automatic transmission option such as was available on the contemporary 300c saloon would have been out of place in a car with the sporting pretensions of the 300Sc, but it does seem a trifle strange in retrospect that the distinctly unsporting column change was not rejected for a floor change like that in the 300SL. The higher performance was matched by standardization of the formerly optional brake servo and by bigger brakes, but curiously, even narrower tyres were specified than had been standard on the lighter and slower 300S. Handling was nevertheless somewhat improved by the addition of the single-pivot swing-axle, which appeared at the same time on the 300c saloons.

However, none of these improvements were visible ones, and the Daimler-Benz marketing people had clearly felt that owners of the 300Sc models should be secure in the knowledge that their cars were instantly recognizable as the fuel-injected variant. The 300Sc accordingly bore horizontal flashes on the bonnet sides similar to those on the 220 saloons, chromed strips along the sills and wheelarch edges, and the full-size chrome wheel trims first seen on the 300b saloon in March 1954. Larger front indicator lenses and swivelling quarter-lights for draught-free ventilation also echoed 300b practice, and there were also larger rear indicator lights.

By the time 300Sc production came to an end in April 1958, sales had dropped to ludicrously low levels after a boom 1956 season in which 140 examples had been sold. The coupe again proved much the most popular model, although the roadster now took second place and the cabriolet thus became the rarest of the 300Sc variants, with only 49 built. The place of the S-models in the Mercedes-Benz range was taken by the new cabriolet and coupe versions of the 220SE, while some sales no doubt went to the 300SL in its roadster guise. Nevertheless, the unique appeal of these beautifully-constructed cars died with them, and with their demise there ended an era which had

The most popular of the three bodies offered on the 300S chassis was the coupe, seen here in 1955 300Sc form, and carrying an almost excessive amount of chrome, so characteristically of the period. Coupes accounted for almost half of total 300Sc production.

begun long before with the great 500K and 540K touring cars.

Specials
The relatively high cost of the 300 and 300S must have helped to keep down the numbers of special-bodied variants, even though the separate-chassis construction made the cars attractive to the specialist coachbuilders in an age when unit-construction was making their art more difficult. Sindelfingen itself built a handful of special bodies on the long-wheelbase 300d chassis for State processional work, and these were known as Pullman Limousines and Pullman Cabriolets. One of the latter was built

for Pope John XXIII in 1960.

Nevertheless, the 3-litre Mercedes-Benz had attracted the coachbuilders' attention many years before the fuel-injected engine and automatic transmission gave the 300d that ability to cruise at walking pace which is essential in a processional vehicle. In all, 16 300 saloon chassis went to outside coachbuilders. Of the 12 300/300b chassis, most if not all received ambulance bodywork by Miesen, or hearse bodywork by Lueg or Kässbohrer of Ulm. The three 300c chassis included at least one kombi by Binz, while the solitary 300d also went to Binz for ambulance bodywork and was delivered to Berne, in

Switzerland.

Farina, in Italy, built a special body on one 300b chassis, although whether this started life as a complete car or was one of the 12 300/300b models delivered in chassis form is not clear. Farina's aim in building the car was doubtless to coax Daimler-Benz into a lucrative contract for the supply of special bodies. The car first appeared in 1955, but was updated twice between then and its final appearance in 1956. In essence, it was a two-door fixed-head coupe with lines fairly typical of Farina designs in the mid-1950s and recognizable as a Mercedes-Benz only by the retention of the standard 300 grille. Stuttgart was not impressed, however, and the car remained a one-off.

Factory records suggest that no 300S or 300Sc chassis were supplied to coachbuilders, but as part of what was clearly a determined attempt to persuade Stuttgart to offer Farina-bodied cars as a catalogued option, the Italian coachbuilder constructed a second special in 1955, this time based on a 300S. It has to be said that the resultant two-door fixed-head coupe was no great beauty, and Stuttgart were right to ignore it. Slightly earlier in 1955, Farina had also modified a 300S cabriolet for a customer in Switzerland, who wanted his car to look like a 1937 Duesenberg. The modifications included a three-position drophead, cutaway front wings, and a spare wheel mounted externally at the rear, but the overall effect was so grotesque that Farina declined even to put his familiar badge on the finished product!

CHAPTER 4

Return of the supercar

The 300SL

The legendary 300SL sports car, particularly in its original production coupe form, has always held a greater fascination for motoring enthusiasts than any other Mercedes-Benz produced since the Second World War. So desirable is the car, and so rarely do any of the 400 or so survivors ever change hands, that the gullwing model has joined the select ranks of those cars which have been flattered by the building of expensive replicas – in this case, a glass-fibre copy powered by a Dodge slant-six engine and built in the USA by sports car specialist Kas Kastner.

What made the 300SL so exciting right from the beginning was that it was actually a racing car adapted for sale to the general public. Its racing career is detailed in Chapter 7; suffice it to say here that Daimler-Benz were determined to restore their prewar reputation through racing, but funds were scarce in the early postwar years and the first car of the racing comeback therefore had to use as many existing production-car components as possible in order to keep costs within bounds. This meant it would have to be a sports/racer rather than a full-blooded Grand Prix car, and that it would have to be built around the biggest and most powerful Mercedes-Benz production engine – the 2,996cc unit of the 300S luxury models.

The biggest problem was that the 3-litre engine was both large and heavy – most unlike the sort of lightweight racing engine that Rudi Uhlenhaut's men would have liked to use as the basis of a competition car. The only possible way around the problem was to make the car ultra-light to compensate. The heavy tubular cruciform chassis of the 300S was obviously not suitable, so the fertile brains at Stuttgart looked around for other ideas. Competitions departments, of course, can get away with ideas which would make production engineers throw up their hands in horror, and Uhlenhaut's team based their new proposal on the example set by recent sports/racing cars from Cisitalia, Aston-Martin and Jaguar: instead of using a conventional chassis, they designed a welded lightweight spaceframe of small-diameter tubes in which, the two cross-members excepted, all the tubes were in compression or tension. The result – a tribute to the hard work put in by Franz Roller's office – was a torsionally rigid and immensely strong structure which weighed approximately 110lb. This was bolted to an aerodynamic body of tightly-fitting aluminium panels drawn up by the designer Paul Bracq, in Karl Wilfert's department. The problem of the tall engine was overcome by tipping it over 40 degrees and mounting it in the frame offset to one side by several inches, a technique seen before in the 1938 W163 single-seater Grand Prix cars. Both open and closed versions of the new W194 sports/racing car were seen during the 1952 season, and their astonishing performances earned for Daimler-Benz exactly the kind of publicity for which they had re-entered the world of international motor racing.

At this point, the 300SL (300 for its engine size, and SL for Sport-Leicht, or lightweight sports) was a pure competition model, and no-one at Stuttgart had even suggested that it might become a production car. Yet Max Hoffmann, the New York agent for Mercedes-Benz, knew a good business proposition when he saw one, and he proposed to the Daimler-Benz management that they should turn the 300SL into a production model. General director Fritz Könecke rather liked the idea,

A 300SL family line-up. From the right, a 1952 works racer, a 1953 pre-production prototype, the 1954-57 production gullwing coupe and a special coupe version of the 300SLR works racer.

The pre-production version of the 300SL, significantly altered from the original competition car, but the gullwing was destined to be changed again before being put into production.

Viewed from the side, the most obvious differences between this pre-production car and the eventual production version are its larger wheels, lack of strakes over the wheelarches and the taller and narrower air vents forward of the gullwing door.

although chief engineer Fritz Nallinger was not keen, and said so, while the competitions people in Uhlenhaut's department had already turned their attentions to the car's 300SLR successor and to the W196 Grand Prix car, and were probably too busy to care. Yet Hoffmann persevered and backed up his suggestion with a firm order for 1,000 300SLs. This put a rather different complexion on the matter. The 300SL was turned over to the production engineers, and they were told to get the car ready for assembly in limited volumes.

The first decision was to use the 300SL coupe as the basis of the production cars, in preference to basing a roadster on the open version. This was partly because the coupe was more familiar, the open cars having raced only once in 1952; but more important was the fact that the closed body could be more civilized inside and would be more rigid. It was already clear that the production 300SL was not going to be a cheap car, and Stuttgart had no intention of compromising its traditionally high standards of comfort and finish! In an attempt to keep costs

to a minimum, the factory did actually experiment with a glass-fibre body, though the project was dropped in 1953 after a single prototype had been built. The first all-metal production prototype 300SL was ready in January 1954, the car was exhibited at the New York International Motor Show the following month, and after a little more development work had been done, the production cars started rolling off the assembly lines in August.

The production 300SL was in fact very different from the 1952 works racers, although it was scarcely less rapid and was considerably better-looking. The original racers had simply been featureless aerodynamic shapes, but the production cars had evolved from the more consciously styled coupe drawn up for the 1953 season but never raced. Without any doubt, the W198 – as the production 300SL was designated – had breathtaking styling, even though it was possible to be hypercritical about the rather dumpy look which resulted from the short wheelbase and big wheels. Its most striking feature

The change in shape and location of the air vents enabled the lower part of the gullwing doors of the production car to be lengthened for easier entry and exit. This early example has a press-button release, which would soon be replaced by a pull-out handle.

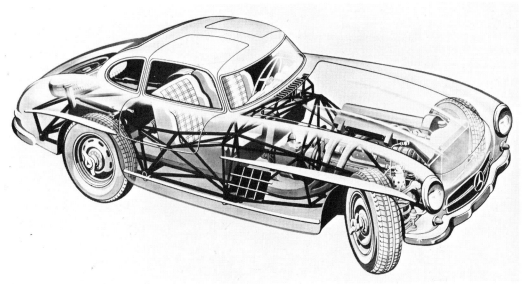

A sketch showing the layout of the multitubular chassis-frame, provision for which had ruled out the possibility of incorporating full-depth conventional doors.

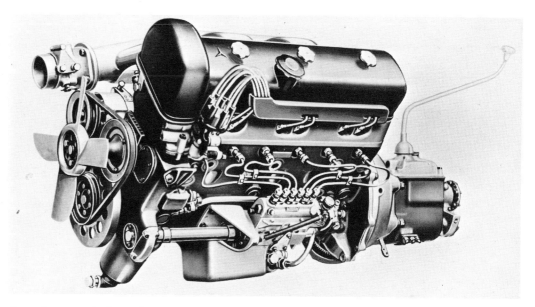

The engine of the 300SL was derived from that of the 300S models, but although those used on the early competition cars were carburettor-equipped, the production 300SL was to feature Bosch fuel injection, giving it a power output of 195bhp at 5,800rpm.

was the doors, which hinged upwards and outwards from the roof panel, and immediately earned the car the nickname Gullwing (the German name, Flügeltür, actually means wing-door). The undoubted aesthetic appeal of these doors transcended the attendant difficulty of actually getting into the car, but far from being a styling gimmick, they were an essential feature because the spaceframe at the cockpit sides had to be deep in order to give strength to the centre-section of the car, with the result that full-size doors were an impossibility. These doors, which had been seen on all the racing coupes from the beginning (though they had been even smaller then, as convenience of entry and exit was a secondary consideration), were the brainchild of Uhlenhaut himself. As there was no way in which the windows could be made to wind down into the lower halves of the doors, the glass was mounted in detachable frames in the production cars, and for open-window motoring the windows could be lifted out and stored in special pockets behind the seats.

Styling changes from the 1952 racers were subtle, but rendered the shape considerably more attractive: strakes over the wheelarches, bigger doors, engine bay air vents in the body sides and twin 'power bulges' on the bonnet were all inherited from the 1953 racing coupe, but the wide grille was a new and neat styling touch which lent an aggressive air to the production cars. Although the racers had all-aluminium bodies, only the doors, bonnet and boot-lid of the standard production cars were aluminium, the rest of the body being steel in the interests both of durability and cost. Nevertheless, after the beginning of 1956 it was possible to buy a special lightweight model with all-aluminium body, which was some 176lb lighter than the standard car, although only 29 such cars were built. The optional centre-lock wheels made production cars look more like the works racers, but the standard wheels were bolt-on, ventilated, steel disc-type, with 300 saloon-type trims. The works racers had all been silver-grey, and this was the standard colour for 300SL bodies, but many cars were delivered in other colours to order. All the bodies, steel and aluminium alike, were hand-built on a slow-moving assembly line at Sindelfingen, and automation only entered the picture when the completed bodies were hoisted on to an overhead conveyor and lowered on to the

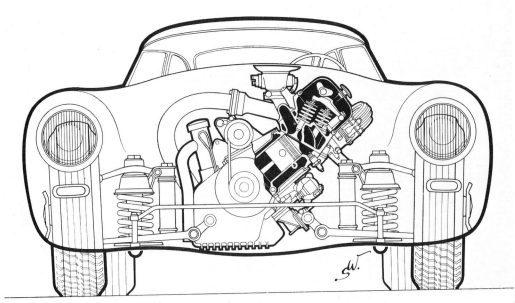

The difficulty of installing a relatively tall engine beneath such low-slung bodywork was tackled by tilting the engine 40 degrees and mounting it slightly offset in the chassis. This drawing illustrates the original racing coupe.

spaceframe and mechanical components, which had been carefully assembled by hand in another part of the factory.

Engines, too, differed from those in the W194 racers. As originally adapted for the 300SL, the 3-litre unit had been given a new camshaft, a higher compression ratio and a new cylinder head, which contained the holes for the sparking plugs, mounted less accessibly in the block of the parent engine. The production cars reverted to the standard camshaft to give them greater tractability in traffic conditions, but they also had a dry-sump lubrication system, a racing feature which ironically enough had never featured on the actual racers! The induction system was also radically different. The first W194 racer had breathed through twin Weber carburettors, and later versions had worn triple Solexes, but the cant of the engine made servicing and adjustment difficult in the extreme because the inlet side of the power unit was effectively underneath. So Stuttgart took a quantum leap into the future with the W198 by fitting its engine with Bosch indirect fuel injection, thus making the 300SL the first production car in the world to be so fitted.

Actually, it was even harder to work on the injection system than on the carburettors of the W194s, but in theory it needed attention less frequently! It also gave the 300SL astonishing flexibility, which was no bad thing for a road-going car. A properly tuned engine would pull strongly and cleanly from around 15mph in top gear, although prolonged traffic work would betray the power unit's racing ancestry when plugs would foul up on occasion.

To contemporary observers of the motoring scene, the use of fuel injection in the 300SL came as something of a surprise, but they should perhaps have remembered that the technology was not new to Mercedes-Benz. The company had long been using injection systems of the indirect type in their diesel engines, and the Daimler-Benz company had gained extensive experience of direct-injection systems through its work on engines for high-altitude aircraft during the Second World War. The Luftwaffe's standard fighter, the Messerschmitt Bf109E, was powered by a direct-injection V12 DB601A engine – and it was considered second only to the Supermarine Spitfire as a fighter aircraft.

The tendency of early 300SLs to oversteer excessively when pushed to the limit was overcome by the adoption of this revised rear suspension incorporating single-pivot swing-axles, as first seen on the 220a saloons, but with the addition of a transverse compensating spring. However, the change had to await the arrival of the roadster version, which replaced the gullwing in 1957.

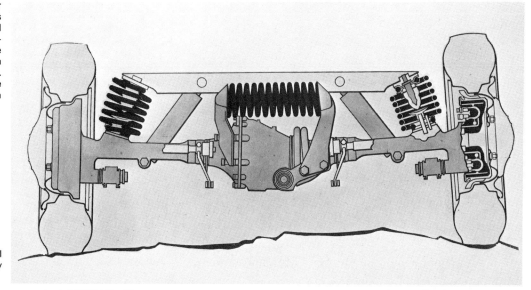

The 300SL gullwing coupe in its final definitive form before being replaced by the roadster models.

The side-boxes in the centre-section of a gullwing 300SL offer the driver a choice of armrest or grab handle according to the mood of the moment.

saloon's brakes were not up to the high speeds of which both racing and production 300SLs were capable, and so massive finned drums of aluminium-iron alloy were fitted all round. These Alfin drums effectively banished fade by ensuring adequate cooling of the brakes, and tremendous stopping power was achieved by harnessing them to a servo. The first 353 production cars had a Treadle-Vac suction servo, but this was linked into the system in such a way that if the servo failed, the driver was left with no brakes at all! Subsequently, an ATE type T50 vacuum servo with fail-safe brake operation was employed. Nevertheless, the 300SL's brakes were still far from ideal: the car had a nasty habit of locking one wheel at a time when braking from high speeds, which made stopping at best untidy and at worst a hair-raising experience.

Although the 300SL suspension was essentially the same as that of the 300 saloons, there were differences between the racers and the production cars, the latter having a slightly wider front track and a slightly narrower rear track. The upper wishbones of what was otherwise the saloon's front suspension were drilled to reduce weight, while the rear suspension was the saloon's double-pivot swing-axle type with chassis-mounted differential, but without the auxiliary torsion bars, and with dampers behind instead of in front of the axles. However, what was just about adequate for a big, heavy, luxury saloon was prone to create power oversteer in a lightweight sports/racing car. While there is no doubt that experienced 300SL drivers could handle their cars without difficulty, a high proportion of customers were rich whizz-kids rather than enthusiasts or racing drivers. Some later 300SLs were fitted at the factory with Michelin X radial tyres, and the combination of these notoriously marginal tyres with the unpredictable back end of a gullwing led Stuttgart to put a 'Do not exceed 120mph' sticker on the speedometers of Michelin-equipped cars!

Exceeding 120mph in a 300SL was, of course, no problem at all. In the standard production cars (a special camshaft was offered from 1956), 195bhp was available at 5,800rpm, and three axle ratios could be had to give maximum acceleration, maximum top speed, or a compromise between the two. The standard 3.64:1 axle gave the best acceleration, with a claimed 145mph top speed. Next up was a 3.42:1 option, giving 155mph, while the third option was a 3.25:1 ratio, which gave

Rather more mundane, however, was the use in both racing and production 300SLs of the gearbox, transmission and front and rear axles from the 300 saloons. The production cars also had the saloon's recirculating-ball steering box, although a rather sharper ZF unit was fitted to the racers. Nevertheless, the

Optional centre-lock wheels helped to enhance the sporting flavour of the 300SL gullwing, while the optional sports camshaft and high-compression head increased power from 195 to 215bhp.

The luggage compartment of a 300SL gullwing was mainly that in name alone, the spare wheel occupying most of the available space.

The hinged steering wheel is a considerable aid to entry and exit with the 300SL, the dashboard instruments of which are sensibly arranged in front of the driver.

all of 161mph. While the actual maxima were hotly disputed, and a May 1955 test by Daimler-Benz on a competition car with a special 3.09:1 axle achieved no more than 155.5mph, acceleration figures were more easily measurable. In all cases, the 0-60mph increment took around 8½ seconds, and 100mph came up in about 12½ seconds more. Such speeds were quite beyond the imagination of the average motorist in the mid-1950s: the family man settled for a maximum of around 70-75mph in his medium-sized saloon, with a 0-60mph time of something like 16 seconds, and the wealthy professional man boasted that his 3-litre luxury saloon could just top the magic 'ton'. Speeds of 150mph and more could only be bettered by out-and-out racing cars: small wonder, then, that the 300SL was

the stuff of which dreams were made!

The works racers had had surprisingly comfortable interiors as a result of Alfred Neubauer's belief that such comfort would improve his drivers' chances in the endurance races for which the cars were entered. Nevertheless, the plaid cloth upholstery of the racers was replaced by top-quality leather in the production cars, and not a little of their extra weight could be attributed to such luxury features as this and soundproofing. The cars remained strictly two-seaters, however, and the space behind the seats was for luggage – of which Stuttgart would provide a fitted two-piece set at extra cost, trimmed to match the seats. Likewise, it was just as difficult to get into a production 300SL as into its racing ancestors – and many owners were

Revised front-end styling with a larger radiator grille, bumper overriders and one-piece light units was introduced with the roadster model in 1957, although US-market cars had round halogen headlamps and a different sidelamp arrangement.

undoubtedly more corpulent than the Mercedes-Benz racing drivers – so the hinged steering wheel of the racers was retained to prevent entry and exit for the driver being a total impossibility.

Once esconced in his bucket seat, he was faced with a pleasantly laid-out dashboard which placed the two large dials of the speedometer and rev-counter directly ahead of him, with smaller dials positioned below them. There was a clock in the middle, and controls for the familiar Mercedes-Benz split heating and ventilating system (not found on the racers) were to be found in a broad chrome band running right across the lower edge of the facia and incorporating various knobs and switches. The central gear-lever with its ivory-coloured knob to match the steering wheel came neatly to hand (though the first 55 cars had

a curious cranked lever instead of the later neat remote change), and the handbrake was outboard of the seat where the high sill prevented it from obstructing entry to the car. All the 300SLs were left-hand drive, the cant of the engine preventing all attempts at a right-hand drive conversion.

The fabulous gullwing Mercedes-Benz was only in production for three years, during which 1,400 cars – not including racers and prototypes – were built by hand in Stuttgart's highest luxury-car traditions. Yet despite the low volume, Daimler-Benz were sufficiently convinced of the value of the 300SL experiment to develop an improved version, and in 1957 the 300SL coupe was directly replaced by the 300SL roadster. Production began in May, immediately after coupe production had stopped, and the cars were available for the 1958

73

season after an initial public showing at the Geneva Show in the spring of 1957 – though the press had been treated to a preview as early as October 1956, when a roadster prototype had been demonstrated at the Solitude race track by Paul O'Shea, the reigning American Sports Car Champion, who had achieved that title in a 300SL gullwing.

Stuttgart had identified certain design shortcomings in the gullwing coupes which it determined to put right with the roadster. These were the difficulty of entry and exit through the gullwing doors, the unpredictable rear-end behaviour *in extremis*, the absence of a sensible luggage boot, and the fact that the car was only available in closed form when its greatest potential market in California would really have preferred an open sports car. It was clear from the outset that costly modifications to the spaceframe chassis would be necessary to provide solutions to these problems, but work started quite early in the gullwing's production run, and the modified roadster chassis was first spotted in summer 1956 at Stuttgart by the German magazine *Auto, Motor und Sport*.

The main alteration to the roadster spaceframe was the provision of a lowered centre section to permit smaller sills and larger doors. Strength was maintained by the addition of diagonal struts bracing these lowered side sections to the rear tubes. At the tail, a further modification allowed the spare wheel to be mounted below the boot floor, thus clearing room in the boot itself for luggage, though there was a penalty in that a smaller fuel tank had to be fitted. Additional changes aft of the centre section permitted the installation of the single-pivot swing-axle rear suspension which had first been seen on the 220a saloon models of 1954. Yet this suspension had an important difference, for mounted transversely above the differential and linked to the two axle halves by vertical struts was a coil spring. As the car rolled on a corner, the spring was unaffected, but when a rear wheel hit a bump, this additional spring was compressed and so added to the stiffness already given by the outboard coil springs. The result was that relatively soft main springs could be used to give a comfortable ride, but cornering behaviour was much improved through what was effectively a stiffer suspension. Coupled with fatter tyres and wider front and rear tracks, this arrangement ensured that the 300SL roadster had none of the gullwing coupe's tricky handling. Unfortunately, its brakes were no better than those of the original production car, despite a bigger servo, and it was not until March 1961 that an all-disc system was introduced. No doubt the cost of modifications to a low-volume model like the 300SL had delayed their introduction, because discs were certainly being tested at Stuttgart when the gullwing had gone into production seven years earlier.

There were other changes beneath the roadster's skin, too. Although the standard engine compression ratio remained unchanged at 8.55:1, US-market models had a 9.5:1 ratio, made feasible by the ready availability in that country of 100-octane

The change to roadster bodywork enabled a wraparound screen to be introduced to the 300SL, while additional chrome included side flashes extending from the air vents along the doors.

In 1958 a hardtop coupe was added to the 300SL range, and at the same time an optional detachable hardtop was offered for the roadster. Relocation of the spare wheel below the boot floor considerably improved rear luggage space compared with the gullwing.

fuel. The raised ratio was good for another 10bhp, which was certainly welcome in a car which had put on a considerable amount of weight as compared to the gullwing model. To maintain acceleration, all roadsters had the special sports camshaft, and the optional lower 3.89:1 axle of the gullwing was standardized for the roadster in the USA, with an even lower 4.11:1 axle as an option; but other cars retained the original 3.64 axle, to which these two ratios plus the 3.42 and 3.25 were optional. Top speeds were not up to those of the gullwing with the lower ratios, 137mph being attainable with the 3.89:1 axle and 129mph with the 4.11, according to Daimler-Benz claims. To be fair, the difference was academic as far as most owners were concerned, but the lower maximum speeds may well have detracted from the roadster's appeal in some quarters.

The increased weight of the roadster – some 250lb of it – was partly due to the revised spaceframe, but more to the extra weight of the convertible top and its associated mechanism. A snug-fitting roadster top which disappeared fully into a well,

75

covered by a neat metal panel, was complemented this time by winding windows, which technically made the car into a cabriolet rather than a pure roadster. From September 1958, it was possible to buy a detachable metal hardtop, which added nearly 90lb to the overall weight, and at the same time a 300SL coupe was introduced with the same hardtop permanently fixed in place. On the roadsters, hood stowage took up all the space behind the front seats, which formerly had been usable as luggage space, so it was just as well room had been made in the boot by putting the spare wheel below the boot floor. As usual, Daimler-Benz supplied a special set of fitted luggage as an extra, and that for the later 300SL models consisted of four pieces.

Though the 300SL roadster and its coupe derivative were closely related to the gullwing coupe in terms of styling, there were important differences. The roadster's long, flat, rear deck was one, and its wraparound windscreen was another. Of course, the doors were deeper and hinged in conventional fashion from the scuttle, while the chrome flashes across the side air vents now stretched across the door bottoms as well to add to the streamlined look. An external racing mirror on the driver's side was standard, while the frontal appearance had been considerably updated by the arrival of what Stuttgart called Lichteinheiten (light unities). These incorporated headlamps, sidelights and indicator lights in a vertical cluster beneath a single large lens, and were the first taste of what would become a Mercedes-Benz trademark throughout the 1960s. American customers, however, could specify a halogen-headlight option, which rather altered the neat frontal appearance.

There were changes inside, too. The minor dials had gone from their positions below the main instrument panel, and were now incorporated in coloured vertical strips between the two main dials – again a foretaste of the practice of the 1960s. As entry and exit were now reasonably easy, the tilting steering wheel was no longer fitted, but the lower sills had prompted the handbrake's move to the centre of the cockpit. Switches were recessed into the dashboard as part of Stuttgart's new emphasis on safety, and a steering column stalk provided a headlamp flasher in addition to indicators, while the wheel now bore a horn ring like that of the saloon cars and was no longer invariably delivered in ivory colour.

The later 300SL was altogether a quieter and more civilized car than the gullwing coupe, and no doubt part of the reason was that it was intended to replace not only that car, but also eventually the 300Sc cabriolet, coupe and roadster, which ceased production in April 1958. Yet the later 300SL lacked the gullwing's competition aura – the factory only built one genuine lightweight competition roadster – and its sales figures were always steady rather than spectacular. Statistics give an accuate rendering of the overall picture: only 1,858 roadsters and coupes were built in six years as against 1,400 gullwings in three years, and the best annual total of 554 for 1957 compares with the gullwing's best of 867 for 1955. An additional deterrent to customers must have been that the cars were some 12% more expensive than the gullwings. Daimler-Benz kept a watchful eye on the market, and when the writing appeared on the wall in 1961 with the introduction of Jaguar's cheaper, faster and more charismatic E-type, plans were made for the termination of production. The last 300SL came off the lines less than two years later, in February 1963.

The 300SL – gullwing, roadster and coupe – did a great deal of good for the Mercedes-Benz image and reputation, but not much for the company's coffers. Once their reign was over, there was no way in which a similar car could be produced again. Daimler-Benz were no longer involved in racing, so there was no convenient racer to use as the basis of a production car; and to develop an all-new car of comparable stature was financially out of the question in view of the small production volumes involved. The 300SL was replaced, like its little brother the 190SL, by the pagoda-roof 230SL – a sophisticated sports car in the Mercedes-Benz tradition, but with none of the 300SL's brute power. After the 300SL had gone, the Mercedes-Benz range was immeasurably the poorer.

CHAPTER 5

The Ponton saloons

The four-cylinder models

The year 1951 was a turning-point in the history of the modern Mercedes-Benz, for not only did it see the introduction of the prestigious 220 and 300 models, but it was also the year when development work began in earnest on the next generation of medium-sized cars. Where the 170, 220 and 300 models had all been based on the cruciform backbone frame of 1930s origin, the new models were to put Daimler-Benz in the avant-garde of motor manufacturing once again by featuring the unitary construction which had already begun to supersede the older separate body-and-chassis designs.

The engineering teams under Fritz Nallinger worked like demons to get the first of the new range – the 180 saloon – into production for July 1953, and it would be surprising if they had not learned all they could from examination of existing German unitary vehicles like Opel's Olympia Rekord, Ford's Taunus 12M and Borgward's Hansa 1500. Yet they also drew on their own experience, and the main strength of the new unitary bodyshell lay in the deep pressings which formed its transmission tunnel and bore more than a passing resemblance to the deep oval tubes of the old backbone frame; but now a sheet steel floor section braced these pressings to closed box-section side-members. To this frame/floor construction was welded the body itself, consisting of sheet and closed steel pressings, plus a roof panel. The resulting structure enjoyed an even distribution of stresses and had great torsional rigidity, which ensured almost total freedom from the squeaks and rattles so familiar in separate body/chassis structures after high mileages had loosened up their joints.

At the front of the bodyshell, the central frame pressings bearing the inner wing panels reached forward to meet a front cross-member, and bolted to these box-sections by one sound-deadening metal-rubber bush ahead of the axle and two behind was a fabricated box-section pressed-steel subframe which carried the engine, suspension and steering assemblies. In the eyes of one German motoring journalist, this so resembled a pontoon bridge slung between the front wheels that he christened the new Mercedes-Benz cars Ponton models, after the German for pontoon. That name rapidly gained currency and was even adopted by Daimler-Benz themselves, so that the range of cars which grew from the 180 of 1954 is now universally known as the Ponton series.

Nallinger's engineers, of course, had not adopted unitary construction because it happened to be fashionable, but because it offered a number of advantages. The absence of a full chassis-frame saved weight and permitted lower body styling, as well as offering new opportunities to minimize road noise transmission. Costs were saved by the ease with which the subframe could be mated on assembly to the engine and front suspension components, and the whole unit then simply wheeled under the bodyshell and bolted up. Conversely, if major work was needed on any of these components, repair costs could be saved by the ease with which the subframe could be dropped from the bodyshell to give first-class all-round accessibility.

Styling as well as structure was new on the 180. It was a low-built, slab-sided design in the contemporary idiom, with the integrated wings suggested only by pressing-lines on the body sides. Yet it was dumpy and homely rather than svelte and streamlined to look at, and the retention of the upright

The arrival of the 180 Ponton in 1953 marked the entry of Daimler-Benz into the manufacture of unitary-construction saloons. However, the 1,767cc engine was an only slightly uprated version of that of the superseded 170Vb, resulting in a relatively modest performance. This is a 1955 model.

This early 180 was photographed by Colin Peck at an enthusiasts' gathering in West Germany. The foglights were not part of the basic specification and the whitewall tyres would not have been available when the car was new.

Mercedes-Benz radiator grille (actually a dummy which lifted up with the bonnet) made the styling look older than it was. Sensibly, the slab sides had not been adopted to the customer's disadvantage, and the wing panels were bolted rather than welded to the main shell in order to minimize accident repair costs. There were practical benefits associated with the new idiom, of course, and interior space actually increased by 22% as compared to the 170Sb, largely because the body was now full-width and the running-boards had disappeared. The three-box styling which had become popular after the Americans took the lead with the 1946 Studebakers also ensured that a large boot was available, in this case some 75% bigger than on the 170/220 models. Both boot-lid and bonnet were counterbalanced for ease of operation, while all the doors were hinged at their leading edges and had pushbutton handles. By later standards, the windows may have been small and the waistline high, but the Ponton body offered a very significant increase in glass area of some 40%.

The 180

The 180 saloon was both the first of the Pontons and – in its final development as the 180c and the 180Dc – the last. As launched in September 1953 to replace the 170Sb model, which it actually undercut in price, it was powered by an improved version of that car's 1,767cc engine. If the fitting of the old side-valve power unit demonstrated that neither the time nor the money had been available to develop a more sophisticated engine, the modifications at least were worthwhile. Tuned for economy rather than power, and capable of running on low-octane fuel, the 180 engine with its higher compression ratio and new carburettor was actually more economical than in 170Sb guise, and could give a remarkable 32mpg as well as a 78mph top speed.

Its 52bhp was transmitted through the same four-speed all-synchromesh gearbox as had been used in the 170Sb, albeit with changed second and third speed ratios, and gear-changing was effected by a similar column-mounted lever. A light and

The front compartment of the 180 on its announcement in 1953. A large-diameter steering wheel has been a characteristic of Mercedes-Benz cars for many years.

One of the first 180 saloons to be supplied with right-hand drive. From 1954 the 180 was also offered in diesel-engined form as the 180D, and although the engine was almost identical to that previously fitted to the 170S-D, the lighter weight of the newer car meant that higher gearing could be used.

smooth-acting clutch took the drive through a divided propshaft to the high-geared hypoid-bevel rear axle and, as usual, top gear was effectively a cruising gear in which acceleration was leisurely. The familiar double-pivot swing-axle rear suspension was employed, with the differential housing this time mounted to the bodyshell by a single sound-deadening rubber block, while rubber-bushed radius arms between the bodyshell and axle casing controlled the latter's movements. This was probably the worst of all the Mercedes-Benz swing-axle designs, but the 180's performance was fortunately not exciting enough to provoke the infamous rear-end breakaway in fast corners very often! Front suspension was essentially inherited from the 170Sb, with unequal-length wishbones and double-acting telescopic dampers running through rubber-mounted coil springs.

As for the brakes, Nallinger's men really had tried to improve on the 170/220 set-up with wider twin leading shoes in the front drums and leading-and-trailing shoes at the rear, but unfortunately the 13in wheels brought with them smaller-diameter brake drums and consequently less opportunity for

heat dissipation, with the result that the 180 was very prone to brake fade. Worse, high pedal pressures were still necessary and contemporary road-testers complained of a tendency for one wheel to lock. Steering was no great improvement on earlier practice, either, for although the recirculating-ball system was lighter than before, it was also noticeably vague about the straight-ahead position.

The central lubrication system had finally gone, to be replaced by an instruction to grease 19 points on the car every 1,250 miles – something which motorists in the 1950s were quite prepared to tolerate. They were no longer prepared to do without heating, however, and the 180 had independently controlled driver's and passenger's heater units as standard. Demister nozzles at the ends of the dashboard were intended to clear the side windows, but were barely effective without the optional blower. Instruments and controls were neatly laid out, with a large round speedometer directly ahead of the driver, which also offered a conservative guide to maximum permissible speeds in the indirect gears. Flanking this were smaller rectangular gauges for water temperature, oil pressure and fuel level, but other functions were reduced to simple warning lights, among which was a low-fuel light to warn the driver to switch to the 1¼-gallon reserve tank. The two-spoke steering wheel still bore the chromed horn ring which operated the turn indicators, and these were still not self-cancelling, while the handbrake had hidden itself, American-fashion, beneath the dashboard. Self-parking windscreen wipers were perhaps a modern touch, but the 6-volt electrical system on which they depended was an anachronism by 1953, and the combined indicator/parking lights perched on the front wings just ahead of the windscreen pillars certainly suggested that the principles of modern styling had not been fully assimilated at Stuttgart.

The 180's interior was in general an odd mixture of high equipment levels and spartan finish, and its clock, anti-dazzle mirror, cigarette lighter, three ashtrays and armrests on all four doors were in striking contrast to the heavyweight moulded rubber floor coverings and the absence of either a passenger's sun visor or a lock for the glove box. Upholstery came in wool-cloth or grained leathercloth, and the standard 180 was

delivered as a four/five-seater with individual front seats, but a front bench seat could be specified at no extra cost to make it into an acceptably spacious six-seater, and reclining front seats were available at a price. In the boot, provision was made for carrying a second spare wheel, and a comprehensive tool-kit was standard. A four-piece fitted luggage set was made available in traditional Mercedes-Benz fashion, and other extra-cost options were twin fog-lights, a radio and a fabric sunroof.

Despite such attractive options, the 180 was available only in five sober colours, which reinforced the 'workhorse' image with which it appealed to fleet buyers. In Great Britain, it nevertheless had something of a quality image, which was just as well since it was fearsomely expensive for a medium-sized family saloon at £1,694 0s 10d inclusive of Purchase Tax in 1954. Yet exports were a vital part of its success, and it proved especially popular in countries with poor roads, where its robust construction was highly prized. By the time it was replaced by the 180a model for the 1958 season, 52,186 had left the production lines in Stuttgart – many in component form for final assembly at overseas plants in countries as diverse as India

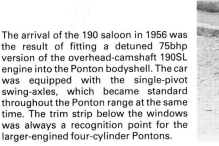

The arrival of the 190 saloon in 1956 was the result of fitting a detuned 75bhp version of the overhead-camshaft 190SL engine into the Ponton bodyshell. The car was equipped with the single-pivot swing-axles, which became standard throughout the Ponton range at the same time. The trim strip below the windows was always a recognition point for the larger-engined four-cylinder Pontons.

81

The 1,897cc overhead-camshaft engine as fitted to the 190 saloon with a Solex downdraught compound carburettor. Maximum power was obtained at 4,600rpm and maximum torque at 2,800rpm.

and the Republic of Ireland.

1954: The 180D

Right from the beginning, Stuttgart had intended to use the Ponton bodyshell as the basis of more than one model, and since Mercedes-Benz were the undisputed world leaders in diesel-powered passenger cars it was obvious that diesel Pontons would be on the cards. The company did not wait until the 170S-D models had outlived their usefulness before introducing the first of these, but launched the 180D as soon as they could. Thus from March 1954 the OM636 diesel engine could be bought in a car which in every other respect resembled the new 180.

The 1,767cc three-bearing engine differed from the 170S-D unit only in its use of tougher bearing material to increase the already legendary durability. However, the 180D was lighter than its diesel predecessors, and so Stuttgart's engineers had been able to mate the engine to high gearing – higher in fact than in the petrol models – without loss of acceleration and with

benefit both to maximum speed and fuel consumption. Indeed, the 180D could return astonishingly good figures in this last respect, 44mpg being a not unrealistic claim. Of course, it *was* slow, taking all of 37 seconds to haul itself up to 60mph from rest and running out of steam at 68mph. It was also noisy, but its combination of low running costs with modern styling and generous interior accommodation made it irresistible to fleet buyers (especially taxi operators) and private buyers alike. To say it was an instant success would be an understatement: in its first year, the 180D accounted for 44% of *all* Mercedes-Benz passenger car production!

For a single season, Stuttgart was content to sit back and watch the booming sales of their three Ponton models – for the introduction of the 180D had been accompanied by the arrival of the 220, the first of the six-cylinder range which forms the subject of the following chapter. The 180D's engine output was then put up by 3bhp for 1956 as the result of an increase in the governed engine speed; but the real improvement to the two four-cylinder models was held over until the 1956 season was

The diesel engine for the 190D was also a new overhead-camshaft unit. It was introduced into the Ponton range in 1958 with Bosch injection equipment and offered 50bhp at 4,000rpm.

already well under way. The 220 had been introduced with an improved version of the swing-axle rear suspension, and from January 1956 this was fitted to both the 180 and 180D models as well.

The single-pivot swing-axle, as the new rear suspension was called, was a development of the set-up first seen in the 1952 W196 Grand Prix car. Where the old system had used a rigidly-mounted differential from which both axle halves pivoted, the revised system had the differential housing mounted flexibly to the underside of the body so that it could swing with the right-hand half of the axle. A single universally-jointed pivot lay low down on the other side of the differential housing, and the left-hand axle half swung from this. The results were a marked reduction in camber change under cornering forces, and a more gradual transition to oversteer which gave the driver more chance to deal with rear-end breakaway, as well as an improvement in rear tyre wear characteristics. If the new system did not completely eliminate the oversteer which a careless driver could provoke from the swing-axles, it certainly protected him from disaster a great deal better than the earlier system had done.

1956: The 190
With sales of the Ponton models booming, Stuttgart was confident enough to introduce three new Ponton models at once in 1956, of which one was a four-cylinder model additional to the 180 and 180D. The arrival of the 190 in May 1956 was accompanied by a cunning piece of price-cutting, for in fact the new car sold at the former price of the 180, and the price of the existing model was lowered. Since the 190 was a better-equipped model, with a larger engine and a number of trim and cosmetic improvements, this meant that both models were extremely competitively priced.

The 190 was sufficiently altered from the 180 to merit the new type designation W121 (the same as that of the 190SL sports car), but it was basically a 180 bodyshell with a detuned version of the 1,897cc overhead-camshaft engine used in the 190SL. In terms of design this was really a four-cylinder variant of the 300 series' M186 engine, and so traced its ancestry back to the early 1950s. With a lower compression ratio than in the 190SL, a milder camshaft and valve timing, different valves and manifolding, and a single Solex carburettor instead of the twins, the 190 engine put out 75bhp. Fuel economy had been one of its design aims, but it nevertheless gave the 190 quite respectable acceleration, plus a maximum speed of 86mph. Like the now superseded 220, the 190 was stopped by finned cast-iron drum brakes, which were additionally cooled by ventilating slots in the wheels (although 180-size wheel trims with a larger central star motif were used), and its improved performance was matched by the single-pivot swing-axles, which would henceforth be standard on all the Ponton models.

A more liberal sprinkling of brightwork helped to distinguish the 190 from its cheaper sister, though fortunately this had been applied with taste and discretion. The car looked wider at the front, thanks to its broader radiator grille, which was flanked by unequal-length bright strips on the air intake vents, with the bottom strip butting against the wing. As on the six-cylinder 220, a slim bright band under the windows and bright rain gutters gave the side elevation a less squat appearance, while front quarter-lights were an addition to the 180's specification. From the rear, bigger tail-light units and huge chromed number-plate lamp housings on the boot-lid made the car recognizable to those not close enough the read its 190 badge. Equipment levels were also up on the 180, with a key lock on the front passenger door and a Sigla laminated windscreen as standard (the 180 now had a toughened-glass screen, the laminated type having been deleted as a cost-saving measure when 180 prices were cut). Interior appointments included a heater blower, a reading light, twin sun visors and coat hooks, while the interior door handles with a small curved pull to release the lock were a further welcome improvement. A headlamp flasher was also standard.

Sales figures rapidly proved that the introduction of the 190 had been a sound move. In addition to notching up substantial home sales, the model proved a resounding export success at a time when success overseas was what Daimler-Benz wanted most. Something over half of all 190s produced were sold outside Germany, and it would be wrong to underestimate the importance of the model in Daimler-Benz's postwar recovery.

1957: The 180a
A whole series of revisions to the existing Pontons were introduced in 1957 for the 1958 season, while prices were kept at their previous levels. In terms of actual production, the 190 was the first car to benefit, although as far as the customer was concerned the revised models all appeared together in the autumn of 1957, details being announced a month before the Frankfurt Show, which opened on September 19.

The major change was to the 180, which was redesignated a 180a when its ancient side-valve engine was pensioned-off and replaced in the 1958 models by a detuned version of the larger-capacity overhead-camshaft unit from the 190. With a lower compression ratio and a single-choke instead of a compound carburettor, 65bhp was available from this 1,897cc unit as against 75bhp in 190 form. This power increase – from 52bhp with the original 1,767cc engine – went a long way towards alleviating the 180's lack of performance, and the 180a was nearly as quick as a 190 while remaining more economical and able to run on cheaper low-octane petrol.

The engine was not the only 190 feature inherited by the 180a, for its broader radiator grille, larger rear lights and overrider-mounted rear number-plate lamps all came from the same source – and in April 1958 the 180a also gained the 190's front quarter-lights – but it was always possible to distinguish the two models because the cheaper car retained the older wheel trims with their small central motif and did not have the 190-type bright trim on its front air intakes. Brighter interior colours and improved seat contours also arrived for the 180a as part of a cross-range policy which took in all the existing Ponton saloons – 180Da (so renamed to keep step with its petrol-engined sister), 190 (which was never renamed a 190a), 219 and 220S – and options now included a key lock on the passenger door, a reversing light, a heater blower, a headlamp flasher, leather upholstery and a fabric sunroof.

By 1957, petrol quality had stabilized in Europe once more, and Daimler-Benz felt able to delete the dashboard-mounted 'octane selector', which had permitted simple retarding of the ignition to cope with poor-quality fuels in the petrol-engined cars. Yet, as many Pontons were sold in export markets where petrol was *invariably* of low octane level, some means of ignition adjustment had to be retained, and so 1958-season models had a vernier adjustment on the distributor itself.

1958: The 190D

The Frankfurt Motor Show had become the traditional launch time for new Mercedes-Benz models, and *aficionados* of the marque were not disappointed when two more Ponton variants were introduced at the 1958 show. The 220SE described in the next chapter was a new top-of-the-range model, destined to be for an exclusive clientele, but the other car was an additional diesel model.

By 1958, although the Daimler-Benz lead in the diesel passenger car field remained undisputed, sales figures had begun to drop, and the 180D now represented only 35.7% of total Mercedes-Benz car production – a substantial figure still, but markedly lower than it had been a few years earlier. It was pretty clear that this decline in market interest could be attributed to the model's distinctly lethargic performance. So a decision was taken to supplement the 180D by a higher-performance diesel model, and Heinz Hoffmann was given the job of developing a diesel unit from the 1,897cc overhead-camshaft petrol engine of the 190SL, in exactly the same way as he had developed the 180D's 1,767cc unit from the old side-

The engine compartment of a 190D with the diesel injectors and pump readily accessible. The lift-up radiator grille forming an extension of the bonnet was to become a standard feature of most Mercedes-Benz models from the 190 onwards.

A 190D demonstrating the slogging performance of its diesel engine. Note the fitment to this 1958 car of the optional folding roof.

valve petrol engine of the same dimensions.

The finished article was known as the OM621 engine. Its block was exactly the same as that of its parent petrol engine, with an oil cooler in the water jacket and an external oil filtration system, but although its overhead-camshaft arrangement was unchanged, the cylinder-head was cast-iron rather than light-alloy and contained the pre-combustion chambers and glow plugs of an indirect-injection diesel engine. The OM621 could muster 50bhp at 4,000rpm, or 7bhp more than the contemporary 180D power unit. Dropped into the Ponton 190 shell as the motive power for the new 190D model, it could hardly be described as a transformation of the diesel-powered Ponton, but it did put acceleration up to levels approaching those of the petrol 180 (itself no road-burner), and it was both smoother and quieter than the smaller diesel power unit.

Generally speaking, the 190D was otherwise quite simply a 190 with a diesel engine. It had a key starter switch with a glow

This photograph by Colin Peck of a 180Dc shows the fatter bumpers and broader grille of the b-suffix and c-suffix cars, which were introduced in 1959 and 1961, respectively.

A four-cylinder Kombi dual-purpose vehicle with bodywork by Binz photographed by Colin Peck at a Mercedes-Benz gathering.

The same camera captured this line-up headed by a Miesen high-roof ambulance based on one of the later broad-grille models.

plug position instead of the separate ignition and starter switches found in the 180D, and it had the 3.7 axle of the 180D, together with that model's plain brake drums instead of the contemporary 190 items. In its original form it only lasted a single season, but as the sales figures of 20,629 show, it was a considerable success.

1959: The 180b, 180Db, 190b and 190Db

Although the six-cylinder Ponton range was cut back to a single model at the close of the 1959 season to make way for the new W111 models, the full four-cylinder range of 180 and 190 in both petrol and diesel forms remained available. All four models benefited from substantial improvements for 1960, and from the autumn of 1959 they were given new designations, all with a b-suffix.

This b-suffix – only the 180a had ever borne an a-suffix – denoted cars with a lower bonnet line and the broader radiator grille of the W111 model 220b, which was introduced at the same time. The fatter bumpers of the new Pontons were also

clearly designed to resemble those of the new W111 model. The 180 and 180D now gained the larger wheel trims of the 190, and all the four-cylinder models were given enlarged rear light clusters, which now incorporated the rear reflectors formerly slung beneath the bumper overriders.

As the W111 models showed, vehicle safety was Stuttgart's latest preoccupation, and the b-suffix Pontons had benefited to some degree from that aspect of the Daimler-Benz research programme. Thus the dashboard now had extra padding and deformable plastic switch gear, while a W111-type steering wheel with padded boss was fitted. This signalled the demise of the familiar horn ring which doubled as a turn indicator control, and now the horn ring operated only the horns, while the indicators were operated by a stalk-type control mounted on the steering column, which also did duty as a headlamp flasher. Doors on all models could now be locked from the inside, and the 180 and 180D were upgraded with neater seat and door trims, and a screen washer was standard (operated by a pedal, which also switched the wipers on if fully depressed). Even the optional extras came in for attention, and what had been a four-

piece fitted luggage set became a five-piece through the addition of a matching hat-box!

The diesel engines of the 180D and 190D remained unchanged for the b-suffix cars, but the engines of both petrol variants were modified. A new carburettor added 3bhp to the 180, while a higher compression ratio for the 190 added 5bhp and around 3mph to the top speed. Although the 180's improved performance scarcely warranted better braking, the stopping ability of the four-cylinder Pontons had always been so poor that it seems unlikely any customers complained about the fitting to the two cheaper models of the finned front brake drums from the 190s – and their addition to the 190D contributed to standardization if nothing else. On the two petrol-engined models, it became possible to specify vacuum-servo assistance as an optional extra, although the insufficient vacuum available on the induction side of the diesel engines denied that option to the 180D and 190D, where it was admittedly less necessary.

During the two seasons of b-suffix Ponton production, sales figures of the petrol-engined versions showed a marked swing towards the cheaper 180, which was a clear reversal of the earlier position. Actual production figures of the 190b at 28,463 were only marginally lower than 180b totals, but averages of 14,000 a year were very much down on the 20,000 or so average of the original 190. The fact was that the 1960 and 1961 model petrol 190s simply did not offer enough over the upgraded 180 to justify the extra initial cost and higher running costs, and so there were no doubt sighs of relief in the sales and marketing department at Stuttgart when the W110 model 190 came along in August 1961 to replace the elderly Ponton. None of that, however, prevented the 190D in its b-suffix form being a great success, selling 61,309 units in the two seasons of its production as against 24,676 of the contemporary 180D. In earlier years, the 180D had actually sold some 25% more annually than its more expensive sister, but by the standards of 1960 it had become a desperately slow car, while the 190D offered both tolerable performance levels and a higher level of equipment, and in fact represented an extremely good buy.

1961: The 180c and 180Dc

Changes made for the 1962-season Pontons were less significant than usual when a new model designation was allocated, but the 180 sold during the final year of production was known as a 180c. Perhaps the c-suffix was intended simply to parallel the re-engined but otherwise similarly barely altered 180Dc, or – possibly – the 'c' was meant to show that the car was a contemporary of the new befinned 190c W110 model. One way or the other the swansong of the petrol Ponton won no new market, and only 9,280 were made in its single season of production. Visually indistinguishable from the 180b models, the cars nevertheless enjoyed better roadholding through widened rear tracks, and better fuel economy from a new camshaft accompanied by valve-train changes and a new carburettor.

The diesel version, however, sold better until the last, and 11,822 of the 180Dc model were built between June 1961 and October 1962. Like the 180c, it was visually indistinguishable from its predecessor, but it did have an extra 5bhp from its new engine, which was essentially a detuned version of the 1,988cc unit offered in the W110 190Dc and described in Volume 2 of this book. The 180Dc was still no racing car, but the new diesel engine offered further gains in flexibility, and the 180Dc retained its traditional pre-eminence among taxi operators in spite of a price increase, for it was still 1,000 Deutschmarks cheaper than the new 190Dc.

The kombi models

Before passing from the story of the four-cylinder Pontons to that of their six-cylinder brethren, it is worth taking a look briefly at the kombi models – the word means dual-purpose vehicle or estate car – built by independent manufacturers. No small degree of expertise went into the adaptation of the unit-construction frame-floor unit, although Binz, of Lorch, had at least had the experience of performing similar transformations on the separate-chassis 170 models. Christian Miesen, of Bonn, however, was new to the game, at least as far as Mercedes-Benz were concerned. The conversions offered by both firms were approved by Stuttgart, and were sold and serviced through the Daimler-Benz network.

Most of the conversions were fitted out as ambulances, but there were also hearses and a few vans, and prices were between 30% and 50% higher than those of the saloons, depending on the type of body and the internal fittings specified. Production began in 1955 by Binz, but their version was soon joined by Miesen's, which offered a higher roofline and was thus instantly recognizable. Assembly of both versions stopped in 1959, but unfortunately exact production figures are not available. On the bases of figures available for the delivery of frame-floor units from Stuttgart, it would seem that around 4,000 were made. The vast majority stayed within the borders of West Germany.

CHAPTER 6

Extended Pontons

The six-cylinder models

The first six-cylinder Ponton appeared in 1954, only a year after the range's introduction with the 180, and more or less concurrently with the 180D. The new model 220, known technically but never by badging as the 220a, was launched at the Geneva Show in March 1954; full-scale production began in June, and the cars replaced the old W187 separate-chassis 220 saloons in the showrooms for the 1955 season.

Although the 220a shared the construction of the four-cylinder Pontons and resembled them closely in styling, it was in fact a rather better-proportioned car with a longer wheelbase and bonnet. These differences of size earned it the new type designation W180. The extra bonnet length, of course, was to accommodate the six-cylinder engine, while the extra length in the wheelbase was given over to the rear passengers' legroom, and was reflected in the body by wider rear doors. In addition, the rear passengers benefited from a larger rear window than was fitted to the four-cylinder cars.

As they would later do so often, Daimler-Benz used brightwork to help identify the prestige model of the range. Chrome indicator housings on the front wings picked up a theme from the older 220 model (they replaced the ugly indicator housings of the four-cylinder cars), and chrome was used for the drip mouldings, a band below the side and rear windows, and a strip on the rear wing pressing line. These were matched by twin aluminium strips on the sills and an aluminium stone-guard at the leading edge of the rear wing. The radiator grille was broader and more raked, while new full-size wheel trims with slotted rims bore a larger Mercedes-Benz star emblem. At the rear, there were larger light clusters and a bigger chromed boot handle at the bottom of the lid. Twin fog-lights fitted as standard concealed the new air intakes at the front, which were now just above the bumper valance (where they picked up exhaust fumes, dust and mud – which was certainly not the intention!). Front and rear doors all had quarter-lights, those at the front swivelling to give draught-free ventilation, while the fixed panes at the rear enabled the smaller winding windows to retract fully into the doors. The 220a came in five standard colours, of which black was probably the most popular.

If the body of the old 220 had been outmoded, its engine was certainly not, as it had only been introduced in 1951. So the 2,195cc overhead-camshaft unit was taken over for the six-cylinder Ponton model with a few modifications, which added 5bhp and put the safe crankshaft speed up by 20% to 6,000rpm. The major changes were the new light-alloy cylinder head accompanied by new pistons and a higher compression ratio, but there were also a new carburettor and distributor, plus a new camshaft and altered valve timing. Durability had received attention, and a paper-element oil filter was fitted, which had the additional benefit of lowering service costs by nearly trebling the mileage between oil changes. A more powerful water pump ensured that the increase in operating temperatures brought about by the higher engine speeds would be kept under control, and as petrol quality was still very variable in certain parts of the world, a dash-mounted octane selector was fitted. The 220a could run without misfiring on the very lowest grade commercial petrol with its ignition fully retarded, but it could not then be expected to attain the near-100mph maximum speed

Introduced in 1954, a year after the announcement of the 180 Ponton, the 220a was built on a longer wheelbase, offering extra space both for the six-cylinder 2,195cc engine and for rear passengers, as well as achieving better-balanced styling.

possible under optimum conditions.

Like the 180, the 220a had dispensed with central lubrication and now had 24 greasing points in the running gear. The 220a also scored two notable 'firsts', being the first petrol-engined Mercedes-Benz to follow the European trend with a 12-volt electrical system (the diesel models already had them to cope with heavier starting loads), and the first Mercedes-Benz road car to use the single-pivot swing-axle rear suspension already described in the previous chapter. Its clutch and gearbox were identical to those of the 180, although the 220a had higher ratios in the indirect gears and a slightly lower axle ratio. The column shift was also retained, although in the six-cylinder car it always seemed rather more positive. As for the brakes, which were without any doubt the 180's weakest point, the 220a had finned drums all round, supplemented by cooling slots in the wheels and wheel trims, and twin-leading-shoe brakes with their inherent self-servo effect at the front.

To complete its prestige package, the 220a had a higher-quality interior than that in the four-cylinder cars. There was wood on the dashboard and on the door cappings, and a grab rail with coat hooks like that in the 300 series was fitted above the side windows. Rear interior lights and twin sun visors were standard, and the remodelled instrument panel featured a strip speedometer in place of the 180's conventional round dial. The clock in the centre of the dash was now an electric one, and the driver was given an extra lidded glove box on his side of the facia. Options included a screen washer, twin blowers for the heater, a radio (the expensive Becker Mexiko set), a fabric sunroof and the usual set of fitted luggage.

If the improvements introduced during 220a production are any guide to the car's faults, it would seem that the first examples had both stopping and starting problems. From spring 1955, some production cars were fitted with what was described as an experimental 'brake booster', and then, after the Frankfurt Show, an ATE vacuum servo became standard equipment, together with Alfin iron/aluminium drums at the front, which greatly improved both cooling and anti-fade properties. A bigger battery was also introduced for the 1956 season. Though the 220a lasted only one more year – for even better models were waiting to go into production – annual sales

The sleeker lines of the 220a as compared with the 180 are clearly evident here. The foglamps were a standard fitment and the six-cylinder cars could also be identified by the indicator light housings above the headlamps.

Inside the boot of a 220a, a model which set new standards for medium-sized saloons and was widely influential. This picture came from the archives of the Rover Company, who had a 220a for evaluation in the mid-1950s.

averaging nearly 13,000 during the two years of its production were ample demonstration that Daimler-Benz had already produced a winner. These figures were closely similar to annual averages for the 180, which meant they were extremely good for a car in the 220's more elevated market sector.

1956: The 219 and 220S

When the 220a stopped production, it was replaced by not one, but two new six-cylinder Ponton models, which arrived for the 1957 season along with the four-cylinder 190. The point of launching two replacement models was to cater more exactly for the requirements of what Daimler-Benz had identified as the two main types of 220a customer, and thus to broaden the market for the six-cylinder Pontons. The 219 was aimed at the buyer who wanted six-cylinder performance rather than prestige and refinement, and was targetted specifically at Opel's successful Kapitän model; the 220S, on the other hand, was aimed at those who were prepared to pay extra for luxury features and expected a six-cylinder engine as part of the package. Although the 220S was based closely on the

The overhead-camshaft six-cylinder engine installed in the 220a being assessed by Rover. Maximum output of 85bhp was achieved at 4,800rpm.

superseded 220a and retained its W180 type-designation, the 219 was very much a different car and was given the special type-designation W105.

The main reason for this was that the 219 was actually a hybrid, combining the short 180 body with the longer bonnet of the six-cylinder models. Thus although its wheelbase was longer than that of the four-cylinder cars, that extra length lay between bulkhead and front axle, and rear legroom was to four-cylinder standards. Since the engine was the same 2,195cc overhead-camshaft unit as in the 220a and the car was a few inches shorter and therefore lighter than the superseded model, its acceleration was somewhat enhanced, although maximum speed remained more or less the same. However, the smaller petrol tank of the four-cylinder models came with the 180-type bodyshell, and so the car's touring range was less than that of the larger-tanked 220a.

It was not difficult to spot a 219, as it looked rather like a stretched 190, with the same discreet levels of bright trim, and it lacked the twin fog-lamps of the 220a unless these were specified optionally; but the 220S was even easier to recognize,

The interior of the 220a, the dashboard of which, incorporating a ribbon-type speedometer, was to be shared with the coupe and cabriolet models which arrived later. Rubber floor matting was a typical Mercedes-Benz feature at the time.

Broad-band whitehall tyres give this 220a a transatlantic flavour although the car is in fact a right-hand-drive example and UK-registered. Although known as a 220a, this model always carried the '220' nameplate without suffix.

The twin-carburettor 100bhp version of the 2,195cc engine as fitted to 220S models installed in the front subframe from which this series of cars derived their Ponton name.

as it added to the long-wheelbase 220a body a chrome strip picking out the front wing pressing line. Its principal difference from the old 220a lay in its engine, which was now equipped with twin Solex carburettors and put out 100bhp – 'more power than you need', as Mercedes-Benz advertisements had it. The peak of the torque curve had risen by 900rpm, and the engine was both more flexible and more economical than the single-carburettor 219/220a unit. In addition, smoother running was ensured by a new four-point mounting between engine and subframe.

The 220S was a very quick car by the standards of the day, with a genuine 100mph capability in the right conditions. Yet Daimler-Benz had followed the American example for their prestige Ponton model, and its soft springing gave a boulevard ride at the expense of handling. The 220S rolled prodigiously on corners and dipped its nose markedly under braking. Fortunately, wider tyres than on the 219/220a models kept roadholding at a high standard within the limitations of the single-pivot swing-axle. Equipment levels were as for the 220a, plus a headlamp flasher as standard, but the options now included a central rear armrest, 21 special order colours in addition to the five standard paint finishes, and 26 two-tone

The 220S saloon is immediately identifiable from its 220a counterpart by the use of additional chrome to emphasize the double curve of the front wings.

The excellent proportions of the 220S are seen to good effect in this side view. The narrow-band whitewall tyres compare favourably with those fitted to the car pictured on page 94.

An interesting picture by Colin Peck showing the post-1957 rear lamps on a 180c alongside the pre-1957 type on a 220S. By the time the 180c was built the four-cylinder Pontons had inherited the larger rear windows originally confined to the six-cylinder models.

colour combinations. In spite of its undoubted faults, the 220S was pretty well without rivals in its class, and it rapidly became acknowledged as the standard by which all other medium-sized six-cylinder European cars were judged. Meanwhile, the 219 enjoyed immense success in overseas markets, and between them, the 219 and 220S put up sales of the six-cylinder Pontons by an average of around 17% annually.

Like the four-cylinder models, the 219 and 220S benefited from a series of improvements in autumn 1957 for the 1958 season. New seats and trim colours arrived, plus a collection of new options already detailed in the last chapter, and the octane selector disappeared from the dashboard to be replaced by a vernier adjustment on the distributor. Paralleling the changes to the 180, both six-cylinder models were also given uprated power units. Higher compression ratios put the 219 engine's output up from 85bhp to 90bhp and the 220S unit's from 100bhp to 106bhp, though Daimler-Benz followed their usual conservative policy and declined to mention the increased maximum speed of the 220S in their publicity literature. The 219, however, was given the higher 3.9:1 axle ratio of the 190SL sports car and altered gearbox ratios to produce not only more speed in keeping with its role as the sporting six-cylinder Ponton, but also improved fuel consumption. Both the six-

In 1956 the Ponton range was extended by the introduction of the 219, a hybrid model combining the shorter passenger compartment of the 180 with the longer front section necessary to accommodate the six-cylinder engine. The low-mounted air intakes flanking the grille can be seen in this picture, although often they were masked by foglamps.

cylinder models had uprated rear dampers, and both could be fitted with the new Hydrak automatic clutch.

The Hydrak was a device made by Fichtel and Sachs which gave the benefits of two-pedal control while retaining the standard four-speed manual gearbox. As such, it was typical of European attempts in the late 1950s to eliminate the clutch pedal on cars whose engine characteristics were not suitable for the fully-automatic transmissions then available. Basically, the Hydrak consisted of an orthodox clutch, which was operated by a vacuum servo as a consequence of pressure on the gear-change lever. This in itself was nothing very new, and indeed the first American automatic transmission developed by Chrysler had followed similar principles; but what was interesting was the use of a torque convertor to take up the drive progressively, plus a switch on the flexibly-mounted final-drive unit which controlled the rate of clutch engagement according to whether the car was accelerating (when the final-drive would move backwards) or decelerating (when it would move forwards). A freewheel in the driveline turned back-to-front also locked-up on the overrun to give engine braking. The concept of the

Hydrak was fine, and the use of the torque convertor did not harm performance too much through the inevitable slip, but unfortunately the Stuttgart engineers had not counted on the driving habits of the average owner. It was important to remember to lift the foot from the accelerator pedal when changing gear, just as in a normal three-pedal car, and failure to do so could produce some interesting kangaroo effects and rapid wear on the clutch friction lining. Likewise, a hand carelessly left on the gear-lever would actuate the clutch, with similarly undesirable effects, and although the Hydrak was a popular option on its introduction, cars fitted with it were difficult to sell on the secondhand market in later years.

1958: The 220SE
Capitalizing on the sales success of the 219 and 220S, Stuttgart launched a new top-of-the-range six-cylinder model at the 1958 Frankfurt Show. Called the 220SE, it survived only a single season, but it was intended at the outset as a low-volume prestige model and to test the market for the planned W111 220SE model. Total sales figures of 1974 – less than 10% of

190D figures over the same period – were consequently no disappointment. In itself, the 220SE marked a notable achievement by Stuttgart, for it was the world's first *everyday* production car to use fuel injection (hence the E in its name, which stood for Einspritzmotor, or injection engine). Allegedly, the Mercedes engineers had turned to fuel injection when all other methods of uprating the 2,195cc 220S engine had failed.

The Ponton 220SE was introduced almost subtly, being an unheralded surprise at the 1958 Frankfurt Show and bearing no outward changes apart from badging to advertise its injected engine. In fact, apart from the engine and a slightly smaller fuel tank, it exactly paralleled the 220S in every way, although the engine differences were enough in Stuttgart's eyes to merit the new type-designation of W128. Fuel injection, of course, was not new to Mercedes-Benz cars, for the technology traced its ancestry to the diesel injection experiments of the 1930s, and through the 300SL of 1954 to the 300Sc and 300d prestige models. Yet, this time, it was applied to the engine of what was basically an upper-crust family saloon to give it a significant performance boost. It was a newer system than those used by Daimler-Benz before, with twin injection pumps working through a distribution system instead of a separate pump for each cylinder. There was also a special control system which

Bosch fuel injection was added to the 2,195cc engine enabling the 220SE model to be announced in 1958 with a power output of 115bhp at 4,800rpm.

Cabriolet and coupe versions were an inevitable development of the Ponton theme, although the extra weight of the two-door bodies made them more suitable for the 220S engine than for the 220 for which they were originally intended. This is the cabriolet A/C layout, which was offered with a choice of bench or individual front seats and either token or proper rear seats.

took such factors as outside temperature into consideration when regulating petrol flow; and in addition there was an overrun shut-off, which helped the specific fuel consumption of the injected engine to be better than that of the lower-powered 220S unit.

Power was increased by no more than 9bhp to give 115bhp at the same 4,800rpm power peak as the 220S, but there were significant gains in flexibility through the massive torque increase from 127lb/ft at 3,500rpm to 152lb/ft at 4,100rpm. Maximum speed was up to 103mph, while through-the-gears acceleration was improved as well. As the performance image of Mercedes-Benz cars in the North American market was a significant asset (the Americans had never quite got over the 300SL gullwing), 220SE models for that market were given even better acceleration through lower ratios in the indirect gears, although the axle ratio remained unchanged. Nevertheless, the Hydrak clutch option was often specified on the 220SE, and this did take the edge off its new-found performance.

The six-cylinder Ponton saloons all disappeared at a stroke with the close of the 1959 season, to be replaced by the W111 six-cylinder models which are dealt with in Volume 2 of this book; 219 production came to an end in July 1959 and 220SEs stopped coming off the lines a month later, although the rather more popular 220S soldiered on until October. Although the four models of the four-cylinder range remained in production, the only six-cylinder Ponton derivatives which survived into the W111 era were the 220SE versions of the two-door models.

Cabriolets and coupes

The two-door Pontons made their first public bow at the Frankfurt Show in September 1955, the open models based on the old separate-chassis 220 having been withdrawn a month earlier. Two versions were announced: the 220A with either bench or twin bucket front seats and an occasional rear seat, and the 220C with a real rear seat. The Stuttgart engineers were no doubt delighted that it had taken such a short time to overcome the problems of making a unit-construction saloon into an open model, for this was the first time they had attempted such a task. To their intense embarrassment, however, the standard 85bhp engine endowed what the catalogues called the 220A/C cabriolet with a performance which scarcely did justice to the car's prestige image. The problem was that the extra reinforcement necessary in the open body had helped to put the car's weight up by 300lb over the equivalent saloon. Despite a flood of orders, management decreed that the model should not be made

A 1955 220 cabriolet with chrome strips accentuating the wing-line and the lower edge of the bodywork including the wheelarches.

Not many 220S cabriolets were made in right-hand-drive form, but this one has survived; it was originally owned by the comedian Max Wall.

A 220S cabriolet with the top up is still an elegant-looking car, as this picture by Colin Peck reveals. Four additional badges attached to the radiator grille testify to the owner's enthusiasm.

available to the public.

Nevertheless, the company saved face as quickly as it was able by starting production of the open car with the more powerful 220S engine about four months after production of the 220S itself had begun. Assembly of a parallel fixed-head coupe began three months after that, in October 1956, with the effect that both models were available as part of the 1957 programme. Two years later, 220SE versions were also introduced alongside the 220S models.

The coupes and the delectable cabriolets were always intended as limited-production vehicles, and were hand-built at Sindelfingen to the very highest standards in the great tradition of the Mercedes-Benz prestige models. There were, of course, differences from earlier practice, for now the craftsmen's skills were devoted to fitting-out and finishing a body which had been mass-produced. Nonetheless, panels were individually fitted to cars in true coachbuilder's style, and this went some way to explaining why the 220S cabriolets and coupes cost nearly 75% more than their saloon equivalents, or nearly as much as a 300c

The 220 cabriolets were almost invariably supplied with contrasting-coloured hoods, this lighter-top example making an interesting comparison with the car illustrated on the opposite page.

Series production of the 220 cabriolet in 1956 was followed three months later by the first of the coupe versions featuring a higher roof-line which terminated in a wraparound rear screen. Another example of a radiator grille indicating enthusiastic club membership. Photograph by Colin Peck.

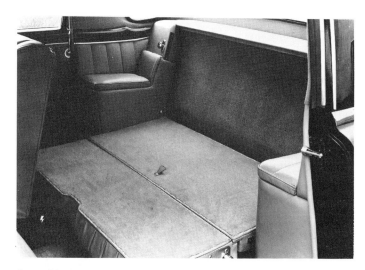

A sensible design feature of this 220S coupe is the fold-flat rear seat, which offers substantially more luggage accommodation when only two people are being carried.

luxury saloon and more than twice as much as a 219! The 220SE models were slightly cheaper in relation to their equivalent saloons, but were very definitely cars for the wealthy connoisseur, classic luxury machines rather than the sporting machines their appearance might have suggested.

The history of the cabriolet and coupe designs can be traced back to 1953, when proposals were drawn up for open models based on the four-cylinder 180. Two variants were considered: a four/five-seater cabriolet B, and a two/three-seater cabriolet A using the same short wheelbase (94½in) as the 190SL sports car, which was then under development. Body styling was essentially that of the saloons, but clearly it was felt at Stuttgart that there was room for improvement and by 1955 there had been radical changes. Quite apart from the fact that the two-doors would now only be made with six-cylinder engines, only one wheelbase length was available. This was nearly 5in shorter than that of the saloons, while the rear overhang had been extended by a couple of inches to give the bigger boot necessary in a touring car and better balance to the overall styling. As far as construction went, the floorpan had been reinforced to help

compensate for the absence of a roof in the cabriolet versions, and of course there were only two doors, which were much longer and heavier than those of the saloons, though their steel skins were stretched over lightweight aluminium frames.

The general lines of the two-door Pontons were similar to those of the four-door models, but there were distinct differences. Unlike the saloons, they had a wraparound windscreen, while front and rear wing lines were different, with heavy chrome trim for emphasis, which would be supplemented by an extra fillet ahead of the front wheelarch if two-tone paint was specified. Bright trim also ran around the wheelarches and along the sills, as on the contemporary 300Sc. The rear overhang was noticeably larger than on the saloons, and the wings terminated in huge tail-light clusters similar to those of the contemporary 300d limousine. The cabriolets had a fully retracting hood, which was easy to operate despite its immense weight and looked good either up or down; but the coupe roof was not an aesthetic success, its abbreviated form contrasting incongruously with the otherwise sweeping lines of the body. It was possible to specify the coupe with a sunroof, and many customers did. Interiors were beautifully put together with leather and wood, of course, and for the cabriolet it was possible to order the A (token rear seat) or C (proper rear seat) specification. Front seats on coupe and both cabriolet models could be bench, individual, or individual reclining type.

The extra weight of these prestige vehicles meant that their performance was not quite up to that of their saloon counterparts, and fuel consumption was also worse for the same reason. The cabriolets were the heaviest of all, thanks mainly to their massive hood frame and mechanism; but none of this deterred the buyers, who after all were interested primarily in the quality and exclusivity of the cars rather than in maximum performance. The best sales year was 1959, in which 1,414 220S and 220SE cabriolets and coupes went to their lucky new owners. A total of 3,429 two-door 220S models had been built by the time production ceased in October 1959; 220SE production continued until November 1960, and the 1,200 coupes and cabriolets built in this final season had the 120bhp fuel-injected engine of the new W111 220SEb model (described in Volume 2). A final production figure of 1,942 for three seasons, demonstrates the exclusivity of these models.

CHAPTER 7

Sports car for the masses

The 190SL

It was obvious to Stuttgart that a car as awesomely rapid and expensive as the 300SL was not going to sell in huge numbers, but it *was* going to attract customers into the showrooms. It therefore made sense to develop a companion model sports two-seater which could feed off the 300SL's glamour and would be cheap enough to be affordable. So the 190SL was born.

Despite the link between the two models which Daimler-Benz always did their best to foster, the 190SL and 300SL were actually as different as chalk and cheese. Whereas the 300SL had evolved from the sports/racers of the early 1950s, and thus originated with the development teams headed by Rudolf Uhlenhaut, the 190SL was a mainstream model developed by the production car engineers under Fritz Nallinger. While the 300SL had become a production car more or less by accident and owed relatively little to the 'ordinary' Mercedes-Benz apart from its 3-litre engine and certain running components, the 190SL was designed from the beginning to use as many standard production parts as possible.

Work on the 190SL began in 1952, just before the introduction of the volume-produced Ponton models, and it was constructed on Ponton principles with a welded frame-floor structure and separate subframe. Yet its underframe was not exactly that of the Ponton saloon, for it had a shorter wheelbase which was, not coincidentally, exactly the same as the 300SL's. The open two-seater body which formed a unit with the frame-floor structure was, of course, very different from the podgy 180 Ponton saloon, and had been designed at Sindelfingen by chief engineer Häcker with a marked resemblance to the open 300SL first seen at the Nurburgring in 1952.

It is instructive to see exactly what Stuttgart thought it was building in the 190SL. Sales literature requires a little translation, its repeated references to the 190SL as 'the car of your dreams' which 'has become a reality' being perhaps more accurately rendered as 'a 300SL lookalike which you can actually afford'. Nevertheless, there were more candid and revelatory descriptions in that same literature. The 190SL was never intended to be a sports car in the traditionally spartan sense; that was not the Stuttgart style at all. The point was that the car 'successfully combines the characteristics of a high-performance sports car with the comfort of a touring car, and offers the sporting driver those qualities of acceleration, roadholding, manoeuvrability and exciting top speed which make driving a pleasure and every road a challenge'. The performance case *was* perhaps a trifle overstated, but all too often the 190SL has been criticised for being insufficiently sporting; for being, in a word, too civilized. Yet it was precisely that civilized quality at which Stuttgart had deliberately aimed during the car's design and development.

From the beginning, the car's main market was seen as North America, and so the 190SL was first displayed in prototype form on the Mercedes-Benz stand at the New York Sports Car Show which opened at the beginning of February 1954. Advertising brochures for 'the Sports Car you've waited for' were liberally distributed, but in fact the car was not yet for sale. Stuttgart wanted to be sure they had got it right, and the New York appearance was intended purely to test public reaction. That reaction demonstrated that Mercedes-Benz had indeed got the car basically right, but Nalliger's engineers took note of those

The prototype 190SL, as exhibited at the New York Show in 1954, was somewhat more aggressive-looking than the car which was subsequently put into production. The bumpers would be entirely different, the radiator intake reprofiled and the air intake above it would disappear.

criticisms which were made, and by the time the car was next seen in public, at the Geneva Motor Show months later, it had undergone some quite significant changes.

Without any doubt, some of these were due to a perceived need to make the 190SL look more like its prestigious 300SL stablemate. It was, of course, an open car and not a closed coupe, and its more orthodox construction permitted the use of ordinary doors instead of the gullwing-pattern necessitated by the 300SL's spaceframe chassis. Head-on, however, not much distinguished the two cars. The resemblance was aided by a grille wider on the production 190SL than on the New York Show car, by a more gentle curve to the front of the bonnet, and by the deletion of the prototype's aggressive air scoop. Even the bonnet panel, which on the New York car reached all the way down to the grille, had been shortened to have the same outline as the 300SL's. Yet there *were* differences: the 190SL bonnet

had a single 'power bulge' instead of the two of the six-cylinder car, and its front bumpers could be fitted optionally with overriders whereas the gullwing's were plain. The 190SL was also slightly wider-tracked and was taller by around 2.2in. From the side, the resemblance was less striking, largely because the four-cylinder car had clearly-defined rear wings where the 300SL had none – but even here, the production cars were made to look more like the gullwing through less bulbous styling than on the prototypes and by the addition of the 300SL-type strakes above the wheelarch to match those already seen over the front wheels.

One of the things which Nallinger's men definitely had got wrong on the 190SL prototype was the column gear-change, which may have saved money by employing production saloon parts, but was certainly not to the liking of the American sports car fraternity. They wanted a floor change like the 300SL's and

The engine compartment of the 190SL prototype. On production models the battery would be moved to the right, a different air cleaner arrangement would be adopted and, of course, a different bonnet top would be fitted.

they said so. The production 190SL, therefore, had a central gear-lever to select its four synchromeshed speeds. The prototype's leather-topped facia with speedo and rev-counter directly ahead of the driver were all close enough to the 300SL design to pass muster, and the ivory-coloured steering wheel also gained approval. Fortunately, it was not necessary to put this on a hinge so that corpulent 190SL owners could get into their cars, for the cockpit was distinctly roomy as sports cars went.

Not only was it roomy, in fact, but quite luxurious, and a far cry from the rather spartan open two-seaters exported from Britain which the Americans were buying in their thousands. The 190SL actually had winding windows; its convertible top

was easy to erect or to stow away; and the boot was generously proportioned by any standards. Seats were initially the remarkably comfortable 300SL type, upholstered in cloth, but modified to tip forward and permit rear compartment access. By mid-1956, these had become special-order items, and the standard seats were a heavily padded, opulent looking design, upholstered in MB-Tex imitation leather or available with real leather covering. Usually, twin bucket seats were fitted, and it is doubtful whether many customers opted for the alternative bench seat, while almost as rare was the optional sideways-facing rear seat for one, which was perhaps most fairly described as an 'occasional' seat. Characteristically for a German car, the front footwells had rubber flooring, although the rear was

A single strap supports the raised engine compartment lid on this production 190SL, on which the column shift of the prototype car has been replaced by a central floor shift.

The 190SL's four-cylinder overhead-camshaft engine which with twin Solex carburettors developed 105bhp at 5,700rpm. This was sufficient to give the roadster a top speed of around 110mph, but acceleration was only moderately brisk.

carpeted; and characteristically for a Mercedes-Benz, fitted luggage in vinyl or leather (three pieces for the boot, two for behind the seats) could be obtained. Typically Mercedes-Benz, also, was the fact that the car was beautifully and very solidly built. Paradoxically, therein lay its greatest failing.

The original intention had been to make the 190SL a lightweight machine, which would be able to double as a sports/touring and competition car, but in spite of the use of aluminium for doors, bonnet and boot-lid, the unladen weight was far in excess of the 1,000 kilogramme (2,200lb) design target. At the New York Show, publicity material had claimed that the bumpers were quickly detachable, the windscreen could easily be swapped for a plexiglass aero-screen, the hood and frame could be removed altogether, and special lightweight doors with cutaway tops and without window glass or winding mechanism could be supplied. Unfortunately, even discarding this much weight did not make the 190SL into a viable competition machine, and the aero-screen and special doors remained extremely rare. The evidence suggests that Daimler-Benz themselves were only too aware of the car's performance

The frame/floor structure of the 190SL. Ponton saloons had a basically similar underframe, but with a longer wheelbase. The 190SL's wheelbase was the same as that of the 300SL models.

shortcomings from the beginning: only 53 of the first 60 production cars had the original-specification 3.7:1 axle, a 3.9:1 unit then being standardized and an even lower 4.1:1 'performance' option being quickly introduced.

Nevertheless, the 190SL's engine was actually a much finer piece of engineering than this sad tale might lead one to believe. Intended from the beginning for eventual use in the Ponton saloons as well as the sports car, it was a new four-cylinder overhead-camshaft unit closely related to the six-cylinder 300 engine, and retaining its 85mm bore, but with a shorter 86.3mm stroke to give 1,897cc. In proper competition fashion, lubrication was by a dry-sump system, and there was an oil cooler built into the cylinder block water jacket. As on the 300 engine, duplex roller chains with tensioners drove the overhead camshaft, but unlike the gullwing, the 190SL had its power unit mounted in orthodox vertical fashion. Twin horizontal Solex

An early production 190SL roadster fitted with the optional overriders and wheel trim rings. Note the early 300SL-type seats.

Without the trim rings the 190SL's wheels have an almost 'unfinished' appearance. The strakes over the wheelarches represent a successful attempt to break up what would otherwise have been a rather plain body style.

Large matching speedometer and rev-counter are clearly visible to the 190SL driver, with the smaller dials and all the controls conveniently laid out below. Dashboard padding is continued along the top of the fully trimmed doors to achieve a unified effect.

carburettors were fitted, and power output was quoted as 105bhp. The New York Show car was supposed to develop this at 5,500rpm on an 8:1 compression ratio; the first production cars had an 8.5:1 compression ratio and developed peak power at 5,700rpm, but the same 105bhp was still claimed. The 110mph top speed was quite rapid enough for 1955, even though 0-60mph took over 11 seconds and some less powerful sports cars could embarrass the 190SL at a traffic-lights Grand Prix. Nonetheless, it was essential to make full use of the gearbox to get the best out of the car, and revving the engine hard produced a pleasantly sporting snarl which certainly enhanced the car's appeal. Unfortunately, a rather heavy clutch detracted from the enjoyment so tantalizingly offered by the maximum speeds of 57mph in second gear and 90mph in third; the temptation was always to leave the car in top and just floor the accelerator.

Handling and roadholding, though, were of a very high order. Springing was perhaps rather stiff, but the 190SL was the first production Mercedes-Benz to use the redesigned swing-axles with low-mounted single pivot, and it could be thrown about with a good degree of confidence up to the fairly high limits of its rear-end adhesion. Braking was another good point, with freedom from fade assured by finned drums, plus the option (on early cars – it was later standard) of vacuum servo-assistance. The handbrake buried under the dashboard hardly belonged in a car with sporting pretensions, however, and the steering was also on the heavy side. Yet no-one could fault the 190SL as a rapid, comfortable, long-distance tourer, and it was as such that the car made its mark.

The New York and Geneva Shows had presented the 190SL only in roadster form, but at Frankfurt in September 1955 Daimler-Benz showed three different versions of the car.

The 190SLs were supplied with rubber matting in the front footwells, although the area behind was carpeted. Note the passenger's grab handle above the glove compartment.

From September 1955 the 190SL was offered as a closed coupe and a similar but detachable hardtop could be supplied for the roadster, then in May 1956 all cars received extra chrome along the sill panels and wheelarch strakes.

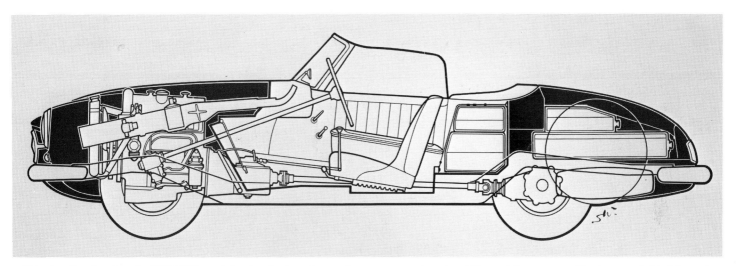

Side elevation drawing of a 1955 190SL roadster showing how the rear luggage compartment could be usefully augmented by the space behind the seats, the compartment in between being earmarked for hood stowage.

Besides the basic roadster, it was now possible to buy a closed coupe and a roadster with a detachable hardtop to the same pleasantly-rounded style as the coupe roof. The coupe was nevertheless destined to be by far the rarest variant, most 190SLs being ordered as roadsters with or without the optional hardtop. Further changes were made in May 1956, when bigger tail-lights were fitted, along with smart chrome trim strips on the wheelarch strakes and sill panels, the latter blending smoothly into stone-guards at the leading edge of the rear wing pressings. A clock was fitted to the glove box lid, which was now provided with a key lock, and the optional brake servo was standardized, along with more powerful horns and a rather feeble heater blower on the driver's side. The chromed bumperettes around the front number-plate also disappeared on home-market cars for 1957, although they continued to be fitted on export models.

The 1958 models which started coming off the lines in summer 1957 had a compression ratio raised to 8.7:1, and benefited from certain modifications which would not appear until much later on the Ponton saloons – indicators now operated by a stalk instead of by the horn ring, and the rear number-plate lights formerly on the body now repositioned on the bumper overriders. Some of the later 1958 cars had a steering lock, and this was standardized about a year later. 1959-season cars were recognizable by their amber front indicator lenses in place of the earlier clear ones.

The autumn of 1959, of course, was the time when Daimler-Benz introduced their new medium-sized W111 saloon (described in Volume 2 of this history), and several changes were made to existing models to add to the publicity splash. The 1960-model 190SL was given an attractive panoramic rear window for its coupe and roadster hardtops, and additionally a wider rear window in its roadster hood. Leather upholstery was standardized on coupe models, and the formerly optional windscreen washer became standard on all three variants. The compression ratio went up again, to 8.8:1, but still the same 105bhp was claimed.

Even though the 190SL had by now earned itself the perhaps undesirable reputation of a 'soft' sports car, these changes seemed to boost sales and more 190SLs were sold during 1960

The passenger compartment of a 1958 190SL; changes from the specification of earlier cars include different bucket-type seats and a clock on the lid of the glove compartment, which could now be locked.

A left-hand-drive but UK-registered 190SL with twin auxiliary driving lamps, but without the bumper overriders which would have intruded in front of them.

The same car, but with the hood erected,
viewed from the three-quarter front . . .

. . . and from the three-quarter rear, where
the hood is seen to have a sensibly large
transparent panel.

Towards the end of 1959 further changes were made to the 190SL range, including the introduction of a revised hardtop for the coupe and as an option for the roadster, which greatly improved rear and three-quarter vision compared with the earlier coupe pictured on page 110.

than in any previous year. Sales dropped off only slightly in 1961, but plans were already afoot to replace the car, and Daimler-Benz decided to quit while they were still ahead. Production of 190SL models for the European market stopped in spring 1962, and although US-market cars continued to come off the assembly lines, there was a gradual run-down of production until the end came in February 1963. Nearly 26,000

190SLs had been built in nine years. It was not a bad start in the luxury sports/touring market, but Daimler-Benz knew they could do better. A month after the 190SL ceased production, the first of the 'pagoda-roof' SL cars was shown at Geneva – and *that* range succeeded in proving what the 190SL had somehow never quite achieved. It is described in detail in Volume 2 of this series of *Collector's Guides*.

CHAPTER 8

Mercedes-Benz cars in competition

1950-1960: SLs, SLRs and single-seaters

Daimler-Benz have always believed in the value of motor sport as a factor in the development of new and better road cars, and after the Hitler War they found themselves severely hamstrung. Germany had been banned from international motor racing, and although the leading personalities at Stuttgart had every confidence that the ban would not last forever, there was simply no money available for a racing programme even to be considered. All Stuttgart's resources were to be poured into getting the company back on its feet and putting a full range of cars into production again, and once finance had been allocated for development of the 220 and 300 models, and for the improved 170 types, there was simply nothing left.

So it is a measure of the importance which Mercedes-Benz attached to motor racing that, as soon as the ban on German participation in the sport was lifted in 1950, they scraped together enough money from their still far from secure company to re-establish their racing department. At its head once again was the former racing driver Alfred Neubauer, whose drive, brilliant organization, and reliance on careful preparation had stood the works team in such good stead before the war and had made Neubauer himself into something of a living legend. On their side, the racing department could also count Rudolf Uhlenhaut, in charge of research and development; and lending encouragement and enthusiasm from above was chief engineer Fritz Nallinger.

Neubauer knew that the only way to achieve the smooth running of the well-oiled Mercedes-Benz competitions machine once again was through actual participation in a race: practice was all very well, but best results were achieved when the adrenalin was flowing. In order to get this team spirit re-established, it was arranged that the works team would enter for two fairly low-key races at the beginning of 1951, and then to take part in the Indianapolis 500 race, which was seen as one of the best ways of getting the Mercedes-Benz name into the public eye of the all-important American market. Stuttgart looked upon America as some kind of salvation, though as yet they did not even have a distributor there to market their products.

The resurrected W154

Of course, there were no cars yet, so three of the prewar W154 3-litre V12 Grand Prix racers which had survived the hostilities were resurrected for the racing department's use. Training sessions began at the Nürburgring in 1950, and cars and team were shipped out to Argentina for participation in the Argentine Grand Prix, held in Buenos Aires on February 18, 1951, and the Eva Peron race, held a week later. Two cars were entered for each race and, despite a good deal of carburation trouble, they achieved second and third places on both occasions behind a much newer supercharged 2-litre Ferrari driven by Jose Froilan Gonzalez. It was the beginning of a running battle between the Mercedes-Benz and Ferrari teams which greatly enlivened the international motor sport scene in the first half of the 1950s. These races in South America were also notable for the first appearance in the Mercedes-Benz team of the Argentinian-born Juan-Manuel Fangio, who went on to become World Champion that year driving for Alfa-Romeo. Fangio came in third behind veteran Hermann Lang in the Argentine Grand Prix; Lang himself then came third in the later race behind Karl Kling,

Daimler-Benz's postwar racing activities began soon after the ban on sports participation was lifted in 1950. Three of these 1939 type W154 3-litre Grand Prix cars were resurrected to take part in a limited programme beginning with the 1951 Argentine Grand Prix at Buenos Aires.

another veteran from the prewar team.

Looked at objectively, these results were astonishingly good in view of the fact that this was the reconstituted team's first race entry and obviously the first time many of its members had ever been involved in international racing. On top of that, it should be remembered that the cars entered were 13 years old! Clearly, Neubauer had drilled his men well, but second and third places were just not good enough. The W154s were simply not competitive any longer. The projected entry in the Indianapolis 500 was withdrawn, and the Mercedes-Benz team was not seen again that season.

Nevertheless, plenty of thought was being given at Stuttgart to future entries. It was agreed during 1951 that the racing department would be provided over the next three years with three new types of car. The first of these was intended to compete in 1952 in races run to the current formula, which was

due to expire after the 1953 season. Partly because of the lack of funds, and partly because its usefulness would be as limited as the formula's life, it would have to use as many production car components as possible. The second would be a full Grand Prix car to race within the new formula for 1954; and the third would be a sports/racer based heavily on the mechanical components of the Grand Prix car. In effect, the team would be getting three cars for a little more than the price of two.

The 300SL
The later road-going development of the 1952 car – the 300SL – has already been described in Chapter 4 of this book. Its genesis, however, was quite simply as planned in 1951: the engine, gearbox and suspension of the new 300S model were wrapped in a lightweight spaceframe bearing streamlined aluminium coachwork styled by Paul Bracq, working under

Rudolf Uhlenhaut, in charge of research and development, alongside one of the early 300SL racing coupes. Driven by Helfrich and Niedermayer, this car came second at Le Mans in 1952.

Karl Wilfert, and the resulting vehicle was race-tuned to the highest possible degree. The result was a closed racing coupe of striking if not particularly beautiful appearance, and weighing no more than 900kg.

The programme of race entries for the 1952 season was chosen carefully: the 300SL would compete in the Mille Miglia and the Prix de Berne in May, in the Le Mans race in June, at the Nürburgring later in the summer, and finally in the Carrera Panamericana in Mexico in November, where it was expected to attract American attention and so promote the Mercedes-Benz name in that country.

Neubauer's racing machine swung into action a full two months before the start of the Mille Miglia, and drivers and pit crews were in residence in Italy practising over the course to ensure that everything went as well as was humanly possible on the day. Three cars were entered, driven by the veteran Rudolf Caracciola with co-driver Paul Kurrle, by Hermann Lang with Erwin Grupp, and by Karl Kling partnered by Hans Klenk. As in the heyday of the Stuttgart team before the war, they raced in all-silver livery. The race was dogged throughout by appalling weather, and although Kling's car was in the lead at Rome, he was eventually beaten by a margin of nearly five minutes by Bracco, driving a Ferrari. Caracciola, who had won the 1931 Mille Miglia in an SSKL Mercedes, was just over 30 minutes behind Kling, in fourth place, but Lang crashed and damaged his car early in the race.

This was not a bad start to the season, but it was not good enough for Neubauer. Two weeks later at the Prix de Berne, held on the Bremgarten circuit, the Ferrari opposition was non-existent when Willy Daetwyler's car broke a half-shaft on the starting line, and Neubauer whipped his cars on to victory, with Karl Kling claiming first place and Hermann Lang second. The third car, driven by Caracciola, came to grief during the race and put its driver out of action with severe leg injuries. Sadly, Bremgarten was to be Caracciola's last drive for the Mercedes-Benz works team.

A first and second were more like it, and Neubauer now set about making sure there would be no mistakes at Le Mans. The first 300SL coupes had featured gullwing doors which opened only down to waist level, but there were doubts whether this

The winning 300SL of the 1952 Le Mans race, which was shared by Hermann Lang and Fritz Riess.

would pass the Le Mans scrutineers – and one is tempted to suggest that the small doors would have slowed the Mercedes-Benz team drivers considerably in the traditional run-and-jump start! So for Le Mans the works 300SLs were given enlarged doors, similar in size to those eventually seen on production models of the car. Tests were also conducted with an air brake mounted on the roof to take some of the strain off the brakes at the wheel hubs, but by the time of the race, the air brake was no longer in evidence.

Three cars were entered, driven by Hermann Lang with new team member Fritz Riess, by Theo Helfrich and Norbert Niedermayer, and by the Kling-and-Klenk partnership which had done so well in the Mille Miglia. The main opposition was expected to come from Briggs Cunningham's coupe and the Talbot driven by Pierre Levegh, but Neubauer had instructed his teams to take it fast and steady and to keep a little in reserve rather than duelling with their rivals. Strict timing was to be observed, and in furtherance of this all the cars ran with a clock and a list of refuelling times on their dashboards. Once again,

Neubauer's thoughtful preparation paid off; although the Kling/Klenk car was forced to retire with dynamo trouble, the other two 300SLs pressed on reliably (the Cunningham ran out of road after only five hours) and were lying second and third – though all of four laps of the Sarthe circuit behind – when Levegh's leading Talbot ran a big-end and dropped out of the race. Lang and Riess went on to take first place, with the Helfrich/Niedermayer car coming in second behind them.

The next appearance of the works 300SLs was in the sports car race which accompanied the German Grand Prix at the Nürburgring. This was the first time the cars had raced on their native soil, and a delighted crowd was able to cheer on their local champions as open versions of the 300SL swept the board in the 3-litre sports car class, with Lang first, Kling second and Riess in third place. A disappointment, though, was the withdrawal after overheating in practice of one open and one closed 300SL with Roots-type superchargers inboard of their triple carburettors; these cars had been entered for the 8-litre class, for under the rules blown engines belonged in this much larger

118

capacity class. Known as the W197, this variant of the 300SL never appeared on a race-track again.

As far as Stuttgart was concerned, however, the climax of the 1952 season was the Carrera Panamericana. This, the third of its kind, was run in eight stages with overnight stops and covered a distance of 1,984 miles. The rules permitted certain modifications, and the 300SL entries all ran with engines enlarged to 3.1 litres. Neubauer's preparation was exemplary, for he was determined to demolish the Ferraris this time. The team practised in Italy to arrive at the best carburation compromise for the tremendous variety of terrain offered by the Mexican race – some sections of the course were over high mountain passes while others were at sea level – and nine tyre dumps were established en route so that the 300SLs could be reshod after every stage with the most appropriate type of tyre for the ground to follow. The careful planning paid off: the Ferrari entries suffered a variety of troubles and the best they could achieve was third place by Chinetti. The 300SL driven by Kling came in first with an average speed of over 102mph, despite being obliged to stop for co-driver Klenk to recover after a buzzard crashed through the windscreen; Lang and Riess were second after damaging their car's body when they hit a dog; and the American John Fitch finished fourth in the only open Mercedes-Benz entry, although he was disqualified for being helped by a mechanic other than Erwin Geiger, who was riding with him.

Thus the 1952 season ended in triumph for Mercedes-Benz, but the company's directors considered that the 300SL had made their point, and announced that there would be no works team for 1953. If this sounds stuffy, it must be remembered that finance was still being carefully controlled at Stuttgart. Although a modified 300SL coupe with a lightweight body and low-pivot swing-axle suspension was on the stocks for the new season, it was never raced, and the next appearance of the works team was in 1954. This brought its own excitement, for it represented the return of Mercedes-Benz to Grand Prix racing, from which they had been absent for 15 years – the 'dummy run' three years earlier in Argentina having been run to Formule Libre and not international formula rules.

The W196 Grand Prix cars

1954 was the first season of the new Grand Prix formula, which set maximum engine sizes of 2½ litres for unsupercharged cars and 750cc for supercharged models. There were in any case numerous disadvantages inherent in a small-capacity engine fitted with a blower, but Mercedes-Benz's main reason for developing an engine to suit the 2½-litre limit was that the lessons learned from an unsupercharged unit were more likely to be of benefit to the company's production cars.

The 2,496cc engine was all-new – a straight-eight with the expected Bosch fuel injection and a tremendously high rev limit of 9,000rpm. In original 1954 form, a maximum of 257bhp was available at 8,250rpm. A system of desmodromic valve gear, which ensured positive valve closing, was employed and, as in some of the prewar Grand Prix cars and the 300SL, the whole power unit was canted sideways in the spaceframe chassis to permit a low bonnet line. A five-speed gearbox was mounted in unit with the differential and the inboard drum brakes at the

The W196 2½-litre Formula 1 car, which marked the Mercedes-Benz team's return to the Grand Prix scene in 1954, seen in streamlined bodywork form.

119

Juan-Manuel Fangio and Karl Kling, who were to finish first and second in the 1954 French Grand Prix, set off alongside Alberto Ascari's Maserati at the start of their debut race with the streamliners.

The W196 in its open-wheeled form, which was to prove the more effective on all but the ultra-fast circuits.

Heading for an historic victory, Stirling Moss leads Fangio in the 1955 British Grand Prix at Aintree. Their cars were only a few feet apart at the finish, when Moss scored his first Grand Prix win.

rear, while extra cooling for the brakes was provided by air ducts in the body. The body itself was not of traditional open-wheeled design, but had been developed with the aid of a wind-tunnel and was not dissimilar to that of the 1938 record car based on a W125 racer. As such, it also carried on the stylistic tradition of the 300SL. Known at Stuttgart as the W196, the new Grand Prix car was tested with the utmost secrecy at Italy's Monza race track.

Meanwhile, Neubauer had been selecting his drivers carefully. Kling and Lang remained from the previous team, but there was a new recruit in Hans Herrmann and the Argentinian Fangio was on the team strength, although he drove a Maserati in some races early in the season. A programme of six Grand Prix events was selected, and Neubauer set about drilling his men with his usual thoroughness.

There were three Mercedes-Benz entries for the French Grand Prix in July 1954, and despite the loss of Herrmann's car with mechanical difficulties on the 19th lap, the Stuttgart team

went home with first and second places, taken by Fangio and Kling, respectively. The same pair drove the two entries in the British Grand Prix at Silverstone, although the result here was very disappointing. Though he had been second at one stage in the race, Fangio was only able to make fourth place at the finish, and Kling trailed him in seventh position.

This was a considerable setback for Neubauer, and it looked as though inadequate preparation had been the cause. The cars were perhaps not best suited to the Silverstone circuit, and they did not give of their best in the heavy rain which had fallen throughout the race. Kling, at least, had no knowledge of the circuit, though Fangio had driven there before. Neubauer was determined that this should not happen again.

The next event on the calendar was the German Grand Prix, in front of a home crowd at the Nürburgring. All four of the works drivers entered, though only Herrmann was driving a streamlined W196 and the other three all had new open-wheel versions of the car. Kling was clearly determined to make up for

The Mercedes-Benz team pose for a picture at the time of the 1955 British Grand Prix, which they subsequently signed. From the left, development director Rudolf Uhlenhaut, drivers Juan-Manuel Fangio, Piero Taruffi, Stirling Moss and Karl Kling, and team manager Alfred Neubauer.

his poor performance at Silverstone, and put everything he had into a brilliant piece of driving during which he broke the lap record on more than one occasion; but after leading for a time, his car developed rear wheel trouble and he had to be content with fourth place. What Neubauer said to him afterwards can perhaps be imagined, because his efforts had overtaxed not only his own car, but also that of Lang, who had spun and stalled his engine while trying to keep up. With Herrmann out of the race after only four laps because of a burst fuel pipe, the team's reputation was left in the hands of Fangio, who – reliably as ever – came in first.

Three cars were entered for the Swiss Grand Prix in August; though Kling retired with ignition trouble, Herrmann came in third behind a Ferrari driven by Gonzalez, and Fangio again carried off first place. Fangio again won at the Italian Grand Prix on the Monza circuit the following month, though the unreliability of his opponents' cars made his task easier than it might otherwise have been. His team-mates fared less well: Herrmann finished three laps behind him after constant pit-stops, though his fourth place was a considerable achievement,

and Kling crashed after a radius rod broke during the race.

The same three drivers entered open-wheel W196 models in the final race of the season – the Spanish Grand Prix at Barcelona's Pedralbes circuit. This time, however, they did not do so well. A high wind blew quantities of dust and rubbish across the circuit, and Herrmann became an also-ran after his car developed clutch slip. Kling drove his boiling car to fifth place, and Fangio managed third despite losing large quantities of oil. Nonetheless, even Neubauer could not complain. The consistently good results achieved by the W196 cars and their drivers had netted Mercedes-Benz the World Championship team prize, and Fangio's brilliant individual performances had made him World Champion for the second time. It seemed like a return to the glorious days of the 1930s, when the Mercedes-Benz name had been on the lips of every motoring enthusiast in the civilized world.

1954 was going to be a difficult act to follow, and 1955 would be a busy season, with the new 300SLR sports/racer becoming available in addition to the W196. As for the drivers, Fangio was an obvious choice, but the performances of Stirling Moss during the previous season had attracted Neubauer's attention, and he was delighted when the young Englishman agreed to join the Mercedes-Benz team as number two to Fangio. Karl Kling, Hans Herrmann and the American John Fitch would also be among the drivers; and there would be other, newer, names.

The W196 cars entered for a full round of Grand Prix events. The first pair were held within two weeks of one another in January in the blistering heat of Argentina. So hot was it for the Argentine Grand Prix that many of the competitors simply collapsed, and of the four Mercedes-Benz team drivers only Fangio – no doubt untroubled by the heat of his native country – managed without a relief. His first place started the season off in appropriate fashion, although it took the combined efforts of Moss, Kling and Herrmann to get the only other W196 to finish in fourth place! The Buenos Aires Grand Prix was run on a slightly altered circuit and to Formule Libre rules, of which Daimler-Benz took advantage by fitting their cars with the enlarged 3-litre straight-eight engine of the 300SLR. The final result of this race was decided on aggregate times taken from two heats: Fangio, Moss and Kling came second, third and fourth in the first heat, and then, after the Stuttgart mechanics had fitted more suitable tyres and had cut holes in the cars' bodywork to keep the drivers cool, Moss and Fangio achieved first and second in the second heat. On aggregate times Fangio was declared overall winner by just 30 seconds from Moss.

The European Grand Prix, held in Monaco in May, was not a good race for the Mercedes-Benz teams, however. Fangio and Moss were using new W196 cars with a short (84½in) wheelbase, but both went out of the race with mechanical trouble. Hans Herrmann crashed his long-wheelbase W196 during practice, so the third position on the team was taken by André Simon, using a spare long-wheelbase W196, but he too was forced to retire with mechanical trouble. By the time of the Belgian Grand Prix, at Spa-Francorchamps a mere two weeks later, Fangio and Moss were equipped with yet another variety of W196 with an intermediate wheelbase length of 86in, and even these differed one from the other for Fangio's car had outboard brakes while Moss' had its brakes mounted inboard. Karl Kling was the third driver this time, in a long-wheelbase car, but he was forced to retire, leaving Fangio to win the race from Moss by a mere 8 seconds.

At the Dutch Grand Prix, in Zandvoort, the finishing order was the same, but Moss succeeded in reversing it in a photo-finish on his home ground at the British Grand Prix, on the Aintree circuit. He and Fangio were this time driving short-wheelbase cars, and were backed up by Karl Kling and Piero Taruffi, who came third and fourth, respectively, with intermediate-wheelbase cars. The final Grand Prix for the W196 – the French and German events having been cancelled following the Le Mans tragedy in June involving a 300SLR – was the Italian race at Monza. As part of the high-speed banked track was included in the circuit, Fangio and Moss were given

The spaceframe chassis of the 1955 300SLR sports-racing car, the design of which was a logical development of the early 300SL.

streamlined cars to drive (the original plan had been for them to use new medium-wheelbase streamliners, though these proved unsatisfactory on test), while Kling and Taruffi drove open-wheelers. Moss and Kling both retired, but Fangio and Taruffi stormed on to first and second places. It was a sterling performance which assured Fangio's World Championship title for the second year running.

The 300SLR

Meanwhile, interspersed with the outings of the W196 had been events in which the new 300SLR cars had been featured. Not unlike the streamlined W196 in appearance, though built on a wider spaceframe so that two persons could be carried if required, they used an eight-cylinder engine of basically similar design to that in the Grand Prix cars, but with the capacity increased from 2,496cc to 2,976cc through larger bores (78mm as against 76mm) and a longer stroke (78mm as against 68.8mm). These enlarged engines produced over 300bhp at 7,500rpm. The 300SLR designation, of course, was a reminder of the close relationship with the 300SL (by now in production), and the extra R simply stood for Rennwagen, or racing car, while the works designation W196S demonstrated the relationship with the Grand Prix cars.

The first appearance of the 300SLR was originally scheduled to be the 1954 Le Mans race, but the cars were not ready in time

A close-up view of the 3-litre version of the straight-eight engine as fitted to the 300SLR and of the car's massive inboard drum brakes.

The 300SLR as originally revealed, with the three-pointed star emblem dominating the air intake and strakes across the air extractor vents along the body sides.

A 300SLR aboard the famous Mercedes-Benz high-speed transporter, which was claimed to be capable of well over 100mph. The sports-racing car has its experimental air brake hoisted.

The brief aeroscreen of the prototype 300SLR has given way to a fully wrapped cockpit surround offering much improved driver protection as well as improved aerodynamics. The metal emblem has been removed from the radiator intake and replaced by a badge above it.

Another variation on the 300SLR theme, this time with the cockpit opened for two occupants and with a headrest behind each seat blending smoothly into the rear bodywork.

Stirling Moss and Denis Jenkinson about to begin their epic run in the 1955 Mille Miglia with their 300SLR, the 722 running number of which indicates their departure time from the starting ramp at Brescia.

One of the 300SLRs as prepared for the 1955 Le Mans race, an event which was to bring tragedy in the form of motor racing's worst ever accident and result in the subsequent withdrawal of the Mercedes-Benz team when leading the race comfortably.

and indeed were not seen in public until testing began at Monza in September of that year. Their first actual race was in the May 1955 Mille Miglia, for which Neubauer had made his four drivers – Fangio, Moss, Kling and Herrmann – practice for months in 300SLs and a single 300SLR. This was the race which made Stirling Moss a hero in his own country and the 300SLR a legend in its own lifetime, for – partnered by British motoring journalist Denis Jenkinson – Moss drove the 300SLR to victory in its first race. Second, after a delay caused by a fuel-injection fault, was Fangio in another 300SLR. Merely stating the results of this race, however, cannot do justice to the Mercedes-Benz triumph. The average speed of 97.7mph which was set by the Moss/Jenkinson car broke all existing Mille Miglia records and was never bettered before the last event was run in 1957; Jenkinson's innovative pacenotes system was a major factor in the victory. Fangio's second place was perhaps less glamorous, but certainly deserving of equal esteem, for he had driven the whole race *without any navigational assistance*.

Four 300SLRs were entered for the Eifelrennen event at the Nürburgring at the end of May, and the German crowd was not disappointed, for Moss and Fangio staged a splendid duel in which the Argentinian beat his team-mate into second place by

a mere tenth of a second, Masten Gregory achieved third place and Karl Kling came in fourth. After this triumph, however, came tragedy. Three cars, all fitted with air brakes developed from those seen earlier on the 300SL, were entered for the Le Mans 24-hour race. Moss and Fangio shared one car, Kling and Simon the second, and the third was driven by John Fitch and Pierre Levegh, whom Neubauer had persuaded to drive for the Mercedes-Benz team on the strength of his heroic single-handed performance in the Talbot at Le Mans the previous year. Two and a half hours into the race, with the Moss/Fangio car lying first and the Kling/Simon car third, Levegh's car collided with an Austin-Healey in front of the pits. The Mercedes-Benz disintegrated against an earth bank, killing Levegh, and its engine and front assembly were hurled into the tightly-packed crowd. Over 80 spectators died, and after a hurried meeting at Stuttgart, the Daimler-Benz directors instructed Neubauer to withdraw the other two cars. Several subsequent international race meetings were cancelled as a result of the Le Mans tragedy, among them the Panamericana road race, for which two special 300SLR coupes had been prepared. Neither of these ever raced, though one of them was used as a practice car for some of the later events.

The racer that got away. Two 300SLRs were built with coupe bodywork, but they were never used competitively.

Rudi Uhlenhaut with one of the 300SLR coupes, which he used for a time as personal transport.

Paul O'Shea racing his 300SL at Riverside in November 1957, the year in which he won the American Sports Car Championship for the third time running.

Karl Kling pausing with his Mercedes-Benz 190D in which he and co-driver Rainer Gunzler won the 8,700-miles Algiers-Capetown rally in 1959.

Yet Le Mans was not the end of the 300SLR's racing career, and Fangio and Moss took the air-braked versions of the cars to first and second places in the Swedish Grand Prix, a tenth of a second apart at the finishing line. At the Tourist Trophy race, held on the Dundrod circuit in September, cars driven by Moss and Fitch, Fangio and Kling, and Count Wolfgang von Trips with André Simon took first, second and third places after the Aston Martin and Jaguar contenders had retired. Yet things were not looking good for the 300SLR at this stage of the season, because Ferrari were leading on points for the Sports Car Constructors' Championship. So Neubauer sent two cars to the Targa Florio, in Sicily, crewed by Moss with Peter Collins, and Fangio with Kling. Their instructions were to win – and win they did. Moss and Collins broke the lap record twice, despite a crash early on in the race, and finished first, nearly five minutes ahead of the second-place car which, of course, was Fangio and Kling's 300SLR. That result was enough to take the Championship from the Italians.

That was also enough as far as Stuttgart was concerned. At the close of the 1955 season, they announced that there would be no more works racing team because there were more important engineering priorities. It was apparent, too, that the Mercedes-Benz name would be kept in the public eye through private

129

Bill Fritschy and Jack Ellis on their way to victory in the 1960 East African Safari with their 219 saloon, with four large auxiliary lamps to help them on their way once darkness falls.

Production cars in competition

Even though the works teams ceased to exist after 1955, and Neubauer himself retired gracefully to take charge of the company's museum at Stuttgart, the nucleus of a competitions department remained active for the purpose of encouraging and supporting private entrants using Mercedes-Benz cars. Karl Kling initially ran this venture, although he was later to hand over the task to Baron von Korff.

Between 1956 and 1958, it was the 300SL which earned most of the glory. Paul O'Shea retained the American Sports Car Championship for 1956 and 1957 with his car, and Walter Schock and Rolf Moll won the European Touring Car Championship in 1956 with class wins in the Acropolis and Sestrière Rallies in their 300SL, a 10th in class in the Geneva Rally with the same car, and a class win in the Monte Carlo Rally with a 220. The team of Mairesse and Génin also took first place overall in the 1956 Liège-Rome-Liège Rally in a 300SL. 1957 saw the 300SL victorious in the Round-Spain Rally and the Caracas-Cumana-Caracas event, and the model chalked up another victory in the 1958 Neige et Glace Rally.

The 190SL was never much of a competition car despite its image, and the only victory of note recorded for the model was in the 1958 Hong Kong Rally. Yet the Ponton saloons *did* develop into formidable long-distance rally contenders, where their robust construction stood them in good stead. Prominent among them was the 219 which was victorious in East African Safari rallies in both 1959 and 1960 with Bill Fritschy and Jack Ellis. The 190 also scored a victory driven by Paulsen and Sommens in the 1959 Winter Rally held in South Africa, while even a 190D, with Karl Kling and Günzler at the wheel, won its class in the African Rally the same year, turning in an average speed of 55.5mph for the 8,727-mile marathon from Algiers to Capetown and drawing valuable media attention to the newly-launched OM621 diesel engine.

In many ways, the rallying achievements of the production cars were quite as important as the more glamorous racing successes, for they were often in less civilized parts of the world, where they spread the name in new markets for Mercedes-Benz to conquer. Moreover, they proved the ability of the cars to survive in tough conditions, something which the racing cars could only hint at.

racing entries: 1955 had not only seen the works team carry off the Sports Car Constructors' Championship and the Grand Prix Drivers' World Championship, but it had also been the year in which Paul O'Shea had won the American Sports Car Championship in a 300SL and Werner Engel had won the European Touring Car Championship with a 220 and a 300SL. The focus was already changing: in future it would be the production cars (suitably modified where necessary) which would fly the Mercedes-Benz flag in competition, and the factory's own records claim 84 victories in 1956, 60 in 1957, 33 in 1958, 32 in 1959 and no fewer than 117 in 1960 (though most of these were by the new W111 220SE model, which falls outside the scope of the present volume).

CHAPTER 9

Buying an early postwar Mercedes-Benz

The choice and the examination

No reader of this book will need to be reminded that durability is one of the essential qualities of all Daimler-Benz products. Nonetheless, it is a sobering thought that the oldest postwar 170 models are now rapidly approaching the age of 40 – which may herald the beginning of life in human beings, but is more likely to bear witness to the ravages of time in cars. The fact that even a Mercedes-Benz can degenerate into a heap of rust is something which has to be faced; and those splendid long-lived diesel engines can eventually burn more oil of the lubricating kind than they do of the fuel kind. So how does the Mercedes-Benz enthusiast avoid buying an expensive liability?

In the period covered by this volume, there is certainly no lack of variety in Mercedes-Benz passenger cars, for the choice ranges from the humble 170D to the prestigious 300S or the exotic 300SL. Yet despite this wide variety of models, only three basic engine families were built at Stuttgart in the first 15 or so years after the war. It will be as well to begin this buyers' guide with a few words on their strengths and weaknesses.

The oldest family is that of the side-valve four-cylinder engines, originally of prewar design, but carried over via the 170 models and the earliest 180 variants until the mid-1950s. Subsequent engines, however, were all overhead-camshaft designs. The 3-litre 'six' introduced in the 1951 300 saloon was closely related to the later OHC 'four' first seen in the 190SL sports car, while the 2,195cc 'six' which also appeared in 1951 was yet another design which was only related to these by certain basic concepts. All the 'fours' had diesel offspring, the side-valve models updated through pushrod-operated overhead valves, but the OHC units differing from their petrol equivalents in little more than combustion chamber design and fuel system. No diesel 'sixes' were ever available, but both the smaller and larger petrol designs were found in a number of different versions, with either carburettors or fuel injection.

In terms of durability, there is nothing to distinguish the side-valve 'fours' from the newer OHC units. All seem to thrive on the three main bearings which in higher-stressed engines would be considered distinctly marginal. The secret, of course, is that these engines were designed to run at speeds high up in their rev range on the German autobahn system; in combination with high axle ratios, this meant that they were very rarely subjected to any kind of serious strain, so that major overhauls are unlikely to be necessary before 100,000 miles or so have been clocked. As for the diesel variants, add 50,000 miles to that, although oil consumption will increase in a high-mileage engine and the familiar diesel clatter will certainly not decrease.

The weak point of all of the four-cylinder petrol engines is carburation, however. The Solex carburettors which were fitted to them were subject to problems caused by wear, and poor starting is a common malady which does not necessarily indicate an engine in need of major work. The problem is particularly acute on 190SL engines with their twin carburettors, on which wear around the throttle shafts makes adjustment and tuning difficult, and idling – in bad cases – next to impossible. In many cases, the diagonal brace which supports the heavy air intake plenum chamber has been removed by an uncomprehending owner or mechanic, so that the full weight of that component rests on its attachment bolts and allows vibration to loosen the gaskets between intake manifold and engine. Obviously, troublesome air leaks are the result. Many 190SL owners have replaced their Solexes with single or twin Weber 40 DCOE carburettors; the twin-Weber set-up certainly gives better performance and trouble-free tuning, but at the expense of higher fuel consumption and more rapid engine wear if the extra performance is used regularly.

The six-cylinder engines are, if anything, even more robust than the 'fours', and should be good for 150,000 miles or so without a rebuild. Solex troubles are, of course, encountered again here, and the alternative fuel injection is not something on which any amateur should attempt to work. Major fuel injection faults are likely therefore to be expensive to rectify. In the 300SL engine, with its higher state of tune, plug fouling and consequent misfiring in traffic are quite common and need not indicate a fault; the trouble should, however, clear itself rapidly with open-road driving.

Turning now from engine types to car types, it is worthwhile to consider availability of the different models as well as their strengths and weaknesses. Anyone who thinks he can go straight out and find a good used 300SL, for example, is in for a shock! Earliest of the cars under consideration here are the 170 and 220 models, which are not plentiful, either in Britain or the USA. There are very few indeed in Britain, although the USA's lack of a dealer network when the cars were current was to some extent offset by returning servicemen who brought examples back home with them from Germany. In continental Europe, however, considerably more will be found, although for the most part they will obviously have left-hand drive. Prices of saloon variants will not be very high, unless a car is in first-class original condition (and even then a seller might have difficulty attracting custom); nevertheless, the desirable cabriolets and coupes will command considerably higher prices almost regardless of condition. In Britain, these are as rare as hen's teeth, but there are far greater numbers in the USA and it is not too difficult to find a choice of examples for sale.

Sadly, it is the two-door models which suffer most in old age, as their wooden body-frames rot and sag, and hold water against the steel body panels, thus promoting rust. Cabriolets are especially prone to rust at the bottoms of their doors, although saloons are far from being immune to the disease. All the 170 and 220 models may suffer from rust at the base of the radiator shell, and likewise the tinworm is particularly active at the point where the front wings rest on their supports above the wheels. These points apart, though, the cars are generally pretty sound, their backbone chassis and separate body making for a long-lived ensemble.

Generally speaking, the 300 models are also long-lived, although rust at the door bottoms and around the wings (especially on pre-300d cars) can present expensive and unsightly problems. The wood trim suffers badly from sunlight, too, and the chromed exterior parts are liable to lose their plating and eventually disintegrate. Rear suspensions on these heavy cars can also become tired. In general, it is not advisable to buy a 300 which needs a lot of work. This comment applies with added emphasis to the 300S cars, which were expensive playthings in their heyday and are extremely expensive to restore properly now. As for availability, neither the 300 nor the 300S sold in great numbers in Britain, although the latter is rather more common on the other side of the Atlantic. Any enthusiast who *really* wants one of these vehicles is advised to seek one in Germany – where, of course, any available will almost certainly have left-hand drive.

The 300SLs are, of course, both very rare and more expensive to buy than any of the other models covered in this book. In Britain, their appearance on the market is so uncommon that any would-be owner is strongly advised to look abroad for a car – all in any case have left-hand drive. Far more will be found in the USA, where the majority of those produced were sold, but even so the would-be owner will have to be patient in waiting for one to appear in the 'For Sale' columns. As for prices, a first-class specimen is likely to cost about as much as a new Rolls-Royce, and anything significantly cheaper should be viewed with grave suspicion. Repairs to a damaged spaceframe, for example, are a specialist's job, and will probably be hideously expensive.

The Ponton models, rapidly becoming an enthusiast's favourite despite their humble pretensions, are fairly plentiful and reasonably cheap on both sides of the Atlantic. In Britain, diesels and four-cylinder cars are very much less common than the six-cylinder models, and the two-door variants are rare (allegedly only 20 RHD 220S cabriolets were built, for example). By way of contrast, the two-door models – cabriolets in particular – are not hard to find in the USA. Two-door cars will be expensive, and it is worth remembering that the doors and front wings of these hand-built bodies were often tailored to the individual car, so that replacing panels can present difficulties.

The more mundane saloons suffer primarily from the enemy of all early unit-construction cars, and rust will render them unlovable if not necessarily unserviceable. Fortunately, the sills are not structural, and rust here need not be too much of a worry, although the jacking points ahead of the rear wheels can also rust out, with consequent wheel-changing problems. The structural tube below the radiator commonly corrodes at its extremities, but other rust traps present mainly cosmetic problems – the inner rear wings (betrayed by water inside the boot), the bottom edges of the doors, the tops of the wings in a line parallel to the bonnet, and directly above the headlamps, where mud collects after being thrown up by the wheels. Doors which shut badly are more likely to indicate hinge wear than body sag, and it is worth noting that front hinges are only accessible after the wings have been removed!

As for the underside, rust may cause the rubber-bushed rear radius-arms to pull out of the floor, while kingpin wear at the front – detectable by rocking wheels vertically to check for excess movement after the car has been jacked up – can be rectified with new parts, though these are expensive. The gearbox has no special weaknesses, although its shift linkage may be sloppy. Clutches unfortunately are not long-lived items, and may have been mistreated in Hydrak-equipped cars.

The basic construction of the Ponton saloons is shared by the 190SL, which is similarly prone to rusting. Rust attacks the sills (again not structural), the jacking point holes and, in bad cases, the structural rails behind the sills. The rear radius-arm attachment points are prone to the same trouble as in the saloons, and the rear inner wings and boot are commonly attacked. Rust will also get at the panels below the headlights, the headlight bowls and the surrounds, as well as the battery box.

Fortunately, about 90% of 190SL parts are still available at the time of writing – though not all from the factory – which makes restoration of a poor example an attractive possibility for those with the time, money and patience. Many 190SLs will be found in the USA, and there is no real shortage of examples even in Britain, where the car nevertheless seems to be somewhat under-appreciated. Prices for good examples are likely to be close to those for similar-condition British sports cars of the 1950s and early 1960s, such as Triumph TRs and MGAs/MGBs.

The foregoing should give some idea of the availability of the various Mercedes-Benz models covered by this book, and of their major weaknesses. Obviously, far more *could* be said about each one, but space is unfortunately limited. The potential buyer is advised to consult other owners of the model of his choice before entering into a purchase and, if he can, to persuade such an owner to accompany him when he views possible purchases. If the purchase goes well, the next step for the Mercedes-Benz enthusiast must be consideration of the problems of keeping the car in good condition, and the next chapter is intended as an outline guide to the available sources of assistance.

CHAPTER 10

In support of the older Mercedes-Benz

Spares, maintenance and the clubs

Anyone who runs and enjoys an older car will be only too aware of the problems which can arise over maintenance and spare parts, but as at least some of those reading this book may be novices to the game, it is worthwhile spelling out the difficulties.

Whereas the owner of a new or recent car can expect to go to a garage catering for the make and find servicing and maintenance expertise readily available, it is a fact that the owner of an older model may go to the same garage and find that the mechanics there have never even seen a car like his before, much less worked on one. Obviously, as age takes its toll and the number of 220S Ponton models (say) on the roads diminishes, fewer and fewer of the cars will pass through a garage's workshops. As the older mechanics familiar with the model move on and are replaced by younger men trained to deal with the current ranges, so an important fund of knowledge and experience is lost.

The situation is similar on the parts front. No competent garage stores man is going to clutter up his shelves with parts for cars which he only sees once or twice a year, because he needs that space for spares for the current models which he sees every day. Likewise, as demand diminishes with the decreasing numbers of a given model in everyday use, so spares are not remanufactured by the factory when stocks run low. The service provided by Daimler-Benz in respect of spares for their older models is considerably better than that offered by many other manufacturers, but the plain fact is that the company claims to provide spares off-the-shelf (or to special order) for cars *up to 20 years old*. That automatically excludes all the models dealt with in this book – although it does not mean, of course, that

Daimler-Benz cannot supply any spares for their older models: many items (generally mechanical rather than bodywork) are still available through Mercedes-Benz distributors in the usual way.

With the servicing and maintenance situation uncertain, and the spares position far from hopeful, the owner of an older Mercedes-Benz inevitably finds himself thrown back on to his own resources. The rest of this chapter is therefore intended as a base for those resources, on which the individual can build.

Without any doubt, the enthusiastic owner of an older Mercedes-Benz should join one of the owners' clubs, because these represent a ready-made fund of advice and help from other owners. Some people seem reluctant to join clubs in case they feel obliged to participate in things which are not to their liking, but this is a short-sighted attitude: while active members are particularly welcomed, no member is ever forced to do anything – and where else can so many people sharing the same problems be found so easily, and for the mere pittance of a year's subscription? It is also a fallacy that the clubs are only for those people lucky enough to own immaculate cars. While most club members do take a certain pride in their vehicles, it is interest in the cars which unites them.

In Great Britain, the club to join is The Mercedes-Benz Club Ltd, whose membership secretary, Mrs Tina Bellamy, can be contacted at 75 Theydon Grove, Epping, Essex CM16 4PX. Like all good clubs, this one keeps its members in touch with one another and with matters of interest through a magazine – in this case an excellently-produced bimonthly publication called the *Mercedes-Benz Club Gazette*. The club also has regional sections covering the South-East, the Midlands, the East Midlands and Scotland, and there are other national sections devoted to the Ponton models and to the SL and SLC models (for which 190SL and 300SL models are obviously eligible). The club has been able to negotiate discounts for members with certain dealers, and there is a full programme of events.

On the other side of the Atlantic, enthusiasts are strongly recommended to join the Mercedes-Benz Club of America Inc, which at the time of writing boasts over 14,000 family memberships throughout the USA and Canada. There are over 70 local sections, all of which have their own social activities and driving events and publish their own bulletins. In addition, there are regional and national events all over the country, and members are kept in touch through *The Star*, the club's bimonthly magazine. This is a really first-class publication, with colour printing enhancing the technical and historical articles, and events and other news. Contact with this active and friendly club can be made by writing to MBCA, PO Box 9985, Colorado Springs, Colorado 80932. As if that were not enough, there also exists in America a club specifically devoted to the 300SL gullwing model, which can be contacted at 1 Lida Lane, Pasadena, California 91103 and, not surprisingly, is known as the Mercedes-Benz Gullwing Group Inc.

There are, of course, many active clubs in other parts of the world, and their contact addresses are as follows:

Australia: Mercedes-Benz Club ACT, PO Box E117, Canberra.
Australian Mercedes-Benz Club, 352 Miller Street, Sommeray, 2062 Sydney.
Super Star Club, PO Box 362, North Brisbane, Queensland 4000.
Mercedes-Benz Car Club, PO Box R122, Royal Exchange, New South Wales 2000.
Austria: Mercedes SL-Club Austria, Hägelingasse 13, 1141 Vienna.
Brazil: Mercedes-Benz Club do Brasil, Rua Visconde de Piraja 284, Apt 504, Rio de Janeiro.
Czechoslovakia: MB-Club Praha, Písecká u. 6, Praha 3.
Denmark: Mercedes-Benz Registret, c/o Poul Jørgensen, Ingeborgvej 25, DK-2920 Charlottenlund.

Finland: Mercedes-Benz Club Finnland, Puotilantie 8 F 99, SF-00910 Helsinki 91.
France: Club Mercedes-Benz de France, 32, rue du Docteur Mercier, 01130 Nantua.
Germany: Mercedes-Benz Veteranen-Club Deutschland e.V., Rheingaustrasse 21, 6802 Ladenburg.
Mercedes-Benz Club Oberschwaben e.V., Schlossstrasse 33, 7955 Ochsenhausen.
Interessengemeinschaft Ponton-Mercedes, Eifelstrasse 18, 5300 Bonn 1.
Mercedes 300SL Club, Münsingerstrasse 66, 7930 Ehingen 1.
Mercedes-Benz Diesel-Club e.V., Hauptstrasse 29, 2211 Huje.
Holland: Mercedes-Benz 170 Club Nederland, Postbus 4275, 3006 AG Rotterdam.
Japan: Mercedes-Benz Club Japan, Masao Kozu, 1581-24 Ozenji, Tama-ku, Kawasaki, Kanagawa.
The Mercedes Club of Japan, 7-6-50 Akasaka Minato-ku, Tokyo 107.
Norway: Mercedes-Benz Klubben Norge, Postboks 540, 1301 Sandvika.
Norges Mercedes-Benz Club, Torgveien 18, 4000 Stavanger.
Switzerland: Schweizer Mercedes-Benz Veteranen-Club, Bläsihof, CH-4624 Härkingen.
Mercedes 300SL-Club, (Etoile Papillon), CH-1271 Le Muids.

All these should prove useful starting-points for finding out where and how expertise and spare parts are available for the older Mercedes-Benz models, but it should be noted that some clubs are unwilling to make specific recommendations about companies. As Donn F. Wald, Business Manager of the MBCA, put it to the author: 'Our club has a legal problem when we recommend a specialist of any kind. A dissatisfied customer to whom we made the recommendation has a tendency to come back to us for help when settling claims. We cannot allow the club to get into a situation of that nature, so we do not make any recommendations or maintain a list of services available'. By far the best method of finding out which companies provide the best service is to rely on personal recommendation from individual club members.

With that *caveat* in mind, there now follows a necessarily brief list of some of the better-known Mercedes-Benz specialists whose expertise may be of interest to owners of those models described in this book. Obviously, this list is purely a guide, and the inclusion in it of a name does not imply any kind of recommendation by either the author or the publisher. In the United Kingdom, full restorations will be undertaken by Doug Elliott Restorations, 11 Sedgemoor Road, Dagenham, Essex (telephone 01-592 0948), but for those whose needs are less ambitious, work of all kinds on Mercedes-Benz cars will be carried out by Petermerc Enterprises, White Hart Garage, Viaduct Road, Chelmsford, Essex. Parts sources include Hans Motors, Cobden Road, South Norwood, London SE25 5NZ; GAT, 81 London Road, Croydon, Surrey; and H.A. Lock, 292 Wellingborough Road, Rushton, Northamptonshire.

In the USA, probably the best-known source of 170, 220 and 300 model parts is Paul's Autohaus Inc, whose Parts Division is at PO Box 978, Amherst, Massachusetts 01004. Specialists in 190SL parts and maintenance or rebuilding work are S+S Imports, 3401 St John's Drive, Dallas, Texas 75205, who can also help with any other Mercedes-Benz model covered in this book. They can be telephoned on (214) 521 8875. For leatherwork, carpets, or soft tops, Bill Hirsch, 396 Littleton Avenue, Newark, New Jersey 07103 can be contacted on (201) 642 2404; panel remanufacturing and paintwork can be done by the Gullwing Service Company Inc, 106 Western Avenue, PO Box 954, Massachusetts 01929, telephone (617) 768 6916; and a place to go for rebuilt engines is Metric Automotive, 81422 Oxnard Street, Tarzana, California 91356, telephone (213) 705 4785. For more major work, there is Scott Restorations, 14661 Lanark Street, Panarama City, California 91402, telephone (818) 787 2881.

Many enthusiasts – this author included – derive as much pleasure from reading about the cars as they do from actually owning and driving them. There is certainly no shortage of material on Mercedes-Benz, but only a small proportion of it can really be recommended. The very best books to date are probably the five volumes by Halwart Schrader and Heribert Hofner, written in German and published in Munich by the BLV Verlagsgesellschaft. These concentrate on the models rather than the history of the Company, and take the story from the 28/95 PS first seen in 1914 to the 450SEL 6.9 of 1980. Volumes 3 and 4 are most appropriate to the period covered by the present book. For those who are more interested in pictures and specifications with a minimum of other text, however, Werner Oswald's *Mercedes-Benz Personenwagen, 1886-1984* is the book to buy. Published by Motorbuch Verlag of Stuttgart, in 1984, it contains an unsurpassed collection of pictures, including rarities and prototypes in some cases never seen before. If the German text is no obstacle, it is worth every penny of its admittedly high price. Another classic is Karl Ludvigsen's award-winning racing history, now only available in its German-language edition *Mercedes-Benz Renn-und Sportwagen*, published by Bleicher Verlag.

In English, the acknowledged classic Mercedes-Benz history is David Scott-Moncrieff's *Three-Pointed Star*, published by Gentry Books, now part of the Haynes Group, although its sketchy coverage of the period since the Second World War is in marked contrast to the detail of its earlier history. Graham Robson's *Magnificent Mercedes*, published by Haynes, is a well-illustrated and very readable history, while among the better monographs on early postwar cars are William Boddy's *Mercedes-Benz 300SL*, published by Osprey, and a pair of excellently-illustrated volumes in the German *Auto Classics* series (with dual-language text), one devoted to the 190SL and the other to the 300SL. For model identification and production data concerning postwar Mercedes-Benz cars, the most useful of a series of books by Robert Nitske and distributed by Motorbooks International Inc, of Osceola, Wisconsin, is *Mercedes-Benz Production Models 1946-1983*. On the racing cars, *Mercedes-Benz Grand Prix Racing, 1934-1955*, by George C. Monkhouse, is an excellent and detailed history published by White Mouse Editions, in London, and Brooklands Books have published a collection of reprinted magazine articles in *Mercedes-Benz Competition Cars, 1950-1957*. Finally, the same company has put out three further volumes of reprinted road tests and articles on the early postwar cars: *Mercedes-Benz Cars, 1949-1954*, *Mercedes-Benz Cars, 1954-1957*, and *Mercedes-Benz Cars, 1957-1961*.

APPENDIX A
Technical specifications

170V, produced June 1946 – May 1950 (W136)
Construction: Oval tubular cruciform-type chassis; separate all-steel body.
Engine: Type M136 4-cyl, 73.5mm bore × 100mm stoke, 1,697cc. Compression ratio 6.1:1 (6.5:1, 1949-50). 3-bearing crankshaft. Single Solex 30 BFVLS updraught carburettor. Maximum power 38bhp DIN at 3,600rpm; maximum torque 72.35lb/ft at 1,800rpm.
Transmission: 4-speed all-synchromesh gearbox with reverse. Gear ratios 4.025:1, 2.280:1, 1.420:1, 1.000:1, reverse 3.72:1. Axle ratio 4.125:1.
Running gear: Independent front suspension with leaf springs; swing-axle rear suspension with coil springs. Piston-type shock absorbers. Worm steering, 14.4:1 ratio. Hydraulic drum brakes on all 4 wheels. 5.50 × 16 tyres.
Dimensions: Wheelbase 112in, front track 51.6in, rear track 51in, length 168.7in, width 62.2in, height 63.4in, ground clearance 7.3in. Weight 2,552lb (saloon). Turning circle 37.7ft.

170Va, produced May 1950 – April 1952 (W136)
As 170, except:
Engine: Type M136 4-cyl, 75mm bore × 100mm stroke, 1,767cc. Compression ratio 6.5:1 Maximum power 45bhp DIN at 3,600rpm; maximum torque 79.59lb/ft at 1,800rpm.
Running gear: Larger diameter brake drums. Telescopic shock absorbers.
Dimensions: Rear track 52.8in, width 64.2in. Weight 2,607lb (saloon).

170Vb, produced May 1952 – September 1953 (W136)
As 170Va, except:
Transmission: Hypoid rear axle.
Dimensions: Rear track 53.5in.

170S, produced May 1949 – February 1952 (saloon); pilot-build May 1949, produced November 1949 – November 1951 (cabriolet and coupe) (W136)
As 170Va, except:
Engine: Type M136 with single Solex 32 PBJ downdraught carburettor. Maximum power 52bhp DIN at 4,000rpm; maximum torque 82.5lb/ft at 1,800rpm.
Transmission: Axle ratio 4.375:1.
Running gear: Steering with 13.9:1 ratio. 6.40 × 15 tyres.
Dimensions: Front track 51.57in, rear track 55.89in, length 175.4in, width 66.3in. Weight 2,684lb. Turning circle 39.37ft.

170Sb, produced January 1952 – August 1953 (W191)
As 170S, except:
Transmission: Axle ratio 4.44:1.
Dimensions: Rear track 56.49in. Weight 2,750lb.

170S-V, produced July 1953 – February 1955 (W136)
As 170Sb, except:
Engine: Type M136 with 6.7:1 compression ratio and single Solex 30 BFLVS updraught carburettor. Maximum power 45bhp DIN at 3,600rpm; maximum torque 79.6lb/ft at 1,800rpm.
Transmission: Axle ratio 4.125:1.
Running gear: 14.1:1 steering ratio. 5.50 × 16 tyres.
Dimensions: Length 175.2in, height 62.6in. Weight 2,684lb.

170D, pilot-build May 1949; produced July 1949 – April 1950 (W136)
As 170V, except:
Engine: Type OM 636 4-cyl diesel, 73.5mm bore × 100mm stroke, 1,697cc OHV. Compression ratio 19:1. 3-bearing crankshaft. Bosch injection pump with pre-combustion chamber. Maximum power 38bhp DIN at 3,200rpm; maximum torque 70.9lb/ft at 2,000rpm.
Weight: 2,750lb.

170Da, produced May 1950 – April 1952 (W136)
As 170Va, except:
Engine: Type OM636 diesel as in 170D, but with 75mm bore × 100mm stroke, 1,767cc. Maximum power 40bhp DIN at 5,200rpm.
Weight: 2,750lb.

170Db, produced May 1952 – October 1953 (W136)
As 170Vb, except:
Engine: As 170Da.
Weight: 2,750lb.

170DS, produced January 1952 – August 1953 (W191)
As 170S, except:
Engine: As 170Da, but maximum torque 74.5lb/ft DIN at 2,000rpm.
Running gear: 5.50 × 16 tyres.
Dimensions: Rear track 56.5in. Weight 2,805lb.

170S-D, produced July 1953 – September 1955 (W136)
As 170S-V, except:
Engine: As 170DS.
Dimensions: Rear track 56.5in. Weight 2,860lb.

220, pilot-build April 1951, produced July 1951 – May 1954 (saloon); pilot-build April 1951, produced July 1951 – August 1955 (cabriolets); produced May 1954 – August 1955 (coupe) (W187)

Construction: Oval tubular cruciform-type chassis; separate all-steel body.

Engine: Type M180 6-cyl, 80mm bore × 72.8mm stroke, 2,195cc OHC. Compression ratio 6.5:1. 4-bearing crankshaft. Solex 30 PAA dual downdraught carburettor. Maximum power 80bhp DIN at 4,850rpm; maximum torque 104.9lb/ft at 2,500rpm.

Transmission: 4-speed all-synchromesh gearbox with reverse. Gear ratios 3.68:1, 2.25:1, 1.42:1, 1.00:1, reverse 3.18:1. Axle ratio 4.44:1.

Running gear: Independent front suspension with coil springs; swing-axle rear suspension with coil springs. Worm steering, 13.9:1 ratio. Hydraulic drum brakes on all 4 wheels. 6.40 × 15 tyres.

Dimensions: Wheelbase 112in, front track 51.6in, rear track 56.5in, length 177.4in (saloon and cabriolet B), 178.7in (cabriolet A), width 66.3in, height 63.4in (saloon and cabriolet B), 61.4in (cabriolet A), ground clearance 7.3in. Weight 2,970lb (saloon), 3,168lb (cabriolets). Turning circle 39.37ft.

300, pilot-build April 1951, produced November 1951 – March 1954 (saloon); produced March 1952 – March 1954 (cabriolet) (W186)

Construction: Oval tubular cruciform-type chassis; separate all-steel body.

Engine: Type M186 6-cyl, 85mm bore × 88mm stroke, 2,996cc OHC. Compression ratio 6.4:1. 7-bearing crankshaft. 2 Solex 40 PBJC dual downdraught carburettors. Maximum power 115bhp DIN at 4,600rpm; maximum torque 114lb/ft at 2,500rpm.

Transmission: 4-speed all-synchromesh gearbox with reverse. Gear ratios 2.95:1 (later 3.30:1), 2.13:1, 1.46:1, 1.00:1, reverse 3.18:1. Axle ratio 4.44:1.

Running gear: Independent front suspension with coil springs and anti-roll bar; swing-axle rear suspension with coil springs and servo-operated auxiliary torsion bars. Hydraulic telescopic shock absorbers. Worm steering, 17.9:1 ratio (from mid-1952, recirculating-ball steering with 21.4:1 ratio). Hydraulic drum brakes on all 4 wheels. 7.10 × 15 tyres.

Dimensions: Wheelbase 120in, front track 58.2in, rear track 60in, length 194.9in, width 72.4in, height 63in, ground clearance 7.3in. Weight 3,916lb (saloon), 4,026lb (cabriolet). Turning circle 41-43ft.

300b, produced March 1954 – August 1955 (saloon); produced July 1955 (cabriolet) (W186)

As 300, except:

Engine: Compression ratio 7.4/7.5:1. 2 Solex 32 PAJAT dual downdraught carburettors. Maximum power 125bhp DIN at 4,500rpm; maximum torque 163lb/ft at 2,600rpm.

Transmission: Gear ratios 3.44:1, 2.30:1, 1.53:1, 1.00:1, reverse 2.78:1.

Axle ratio 4.67:1.

Running gear: Larger brake drums with vacuum-operated servo assistance.

Dimensions: Length 199.4in, height 64.6in.

300c, pilot-build September 1955, produced December 1955 – June 1956 (cabriolet); produced September 1955 – July 1957 (saloon); produced July 1956 – July 1957 (limousine) (W186)

As 300b, except:

Transmission: Optional 3-speed automatic available; gear ratios 2.303:1, 1.435:1, 1.000:1, reverse 2.78:1.

Running gear: Single-pivot swing-axle rear suspension with coil springs and servo-operated auxiliary torsion bars.

Dimensions: Wheelbase (limousine) 124in, length (limousine) 203.3in, height 63in. Weight 4,092lb (saloon, manual), 4,202lb (cabriolet, manual), 4,202lb (saloon, automatic), 4,312lb (cabriolet, automatic). Turning circle (limousine) 42-44ft.

300d, pilot-build August 1957, produced November 1957 – March 1962 (saloon); produced July 1958 – February 1962 (cabriolet) (W189)

As 300c, except:

Engine: Compression ratio 8.55:1. Bosch fuel injection. Maximum power 160bhp DIN at 5,300rpm; maximum torque 175lb/ft at 4,200rpm.

Transmission: 3-speed automatic standard, 4-speed manual available, with 3.08:1 reverse gear ratio, to special order.

Running gear: Servo-assisted steering from September 1958.

Dimensions: Wheelbase 124in, length 204.3in, width 73.2in, height 63.8in. Weight 4,290lb (manual), 4,400lb (automatic).

300S, pilot-build September 1951, produced July 1952 – August 1955 (W188)

Construction: Oval tubular cruciform-type chassis; separate body.

Engine: Type M188 6-cyl, 85mm bore × 88mm stroke, 2,996cc OHC. Compression ratio 7.8:1. 7-bearing crankshaft. 3 Solex 40 PBJC downdraught carburettors. Maximum power 150bhp DIN at 5,000rpm; maximum torque 170lb/ft at 3,800rpm.

Transmission: 4-speed all-synchromesh gearbox with reverse. Gear ratios 3.33:1, 2.12:1, 1.46:1, 1.00:1, reverse 3.18:1; later 3.68:1, 2.25:1, 1.42:1, 1.00:1, reverse 2.78:1. Axle ratio 4.125:1.

Running gear: Independent front suspension with coil springs and anti-roll bar; swing-axle rear suspension with coil springs. Hydraulic telescopic shock absorbers. Recirculating-ball steering, 21.4:1 ratio. Hydraulic drum brakes on all 4 wheels. 6.70 × 15 tyres.

Dimensions: Wheelbase 114.2in, front track 58.2in, rear track 60in, length 185in, width 73.2in, height 59.4in, ground clearance 7.1in. Weight 3,880lb. Turning circle 40-42ft.

300Sc, pilot-build September 1955, produced December 1955 – April 1958 **(W188)**
As 300S, except:
Engine: Compression ratio 8.55:1. Bosch fuel injection. Maximum power 175bhp DIN at 5,400rpm; maximum torque 188lb/ft at 4,300rpm.
Transmission: Gear ratios 3.55:1, 2.30:1, 1.53:1, 1.00:1, reverse 2.78:1. Axle ratio 4.44:1.
Running gear: Single-pivot swing-axle rear suspension with coil springs. Larger brakes.
Weight: 3,924lb.

300SL, racing versions (W194, W197) built 1952; **(W198)**
coupe, produced August 1954 – May 1957;
roadster, pilot-build February 1957, produced May 1957 – February 1963
Construction: Steel tubular spaceframe with separate body of light sheet steel (aluminium body available to order).
Engine: Type M198 6-cyl, 85mm bore × 88mm stroke, 2,996cc OHC (last 229 built with all-alloy block). Compression ratio 8.55:1 (9.5:1 on US roadster models). 7-bearing crankshaft, Bosch direct fuel injection. Maximum power 195bhp DIN at 5,800rpm (US roadster models and others with optional sports camshaft and high compression head 215bhp DIN at 6,100rpm); maximum torque 217lb/ft at 4,800rpm (US roadsters, etc, 228lb/ft).
Transmission: 4-speed all-synchromesh gearbox with reverse. Gear ratios 3.34:1, 1.97:1, 1.385:1, 1.00:1, reverse 2.57:1 (later and all roadsters 2.73:1). Single-dry-plate clutch. ZF limited-slip differential. Axle ratio 3.64:1 (3.25:1, 3.42:1, 3.89:1 and 4.11:1 optionally available, 3.89:1 standard on US-market roadsters).
Running gear: Independent front suspension with twin wishbones, coil springs and anti-roll bar. Swing-axle rear suspension with coil springs (roadsters have single-pivot swing-axle with compensating spring and coil springs). Hydraulic telescopic shock absorbers. Recirculating-ball steering, 17.3:1 ratio (lower and higher ratios available to order). Hydraulic drum brakes on all 4 wheels (disc brakes from March 1961) with servo assistance. 6.50 × 15 tyres (6.70 × 15 on roadsters).
Dimensions: Wheelbase 94.5in, front track 54.5in (roadsters 55in), rear track 56.5in (roadsters 57in), length 178in (roadsters 180in), width 70.5in, height 51.2in, ground clearance 5.1in. Weight 2,890lb (roadsters 3,130lb, 3,220lb with hardtop). Turning circle 37ft.

180, produced July 1953 – June 1957 **(W120)**
Construction: All-steel unitary body with separate front subframe.
Engine: Type M136 4-cyl, 75mm bore × 100mm stroke, 1,767cc. Compression ratio 6.8:1. 3-bearing crankshaft. Solex 32 PICB downdraught carburettor. Maximum power 52bhp DIN at 4,000rpm; maximum torque 82.5lb/ft at 1,800rpm.
Transmission: 4-speed all-synchromesh gearbox with reverse. Gear ratios 4.05:1, 2.38:1, 1.53:1, 1.00:1, reverse 3.92:1. Axle ratio 3.89:1.
Running gear: Independent front suspension with coil springs; swing-axle rear suspension with coil springs (single-pivot swing-axle from September 1955). Recirculating-ball steering, 18.5:1 ratio. Hydraulic drum brakes on all 4 wheels. 6.40 × 13 tyres.
Dimensions: Wheelbase 104.3in, front track 55.9in, rear track 58.1in, length 176.4in, width 68.5in, height 61.4in, ground clearance 7.3in. Weight 2,596lb (2,640lb from September 1955). Turning circle 38ft.

180D, pilot-build October 1953, produced February 1954 – July 1959 **(W120)**
As 180, except:
Engine: Type OM636 4-cyl diesel, 75mm bore × 100mm stroke, 1,767cc. Compression ratio 19:1. 3-bearing crankshaft. Maximum power 40bhp DIN at 3,200rpm (43bhp at 3,500rpm from September 1955); maximum torque 75lb/ft at 2,000rpm.
Transmission: Axle ratio 3.7:1.
Dimensions: Front track 56.3in. Weight 2,684lb.

180a, produced June 1957 – July 1959 **(W120)**
As 180, except:
Engine: Type M136 4-cyl, 85mm bore × 83.6mm stroke, 1,897cc. Compression ratio 6.8:1. 3-bearing crankshaft. Solex 32 PICB carburettor. Maximum power 65bhp DIN at 4,500rpm; maximum torque 94lb/ft at 2,200rpm.
Transmission: Axle ratio 3.9:1.
Weight: 2,662lb.

180b, produced July 1959 – August 1961 **(W120)**
As 180a, except:
Engine: Solex 34 PICB downdraught carburettor. Maximum power 68bhp DIN at 4,400rpm; maximum torque 96lb/ft at 2,500rpm.
Running gear: Brakes with larger swept area and optional vacuum servo assistance.

180Db, produced July 1959 – August 1961 **(W120)**
Technical specification identical to 180D.

180c, produced June 1961 – October 1962 **(W120)**
As 180b, except:
Engine: Improved valve gear.

180Dc, produced June 1961 – October 1962 **(W120)**
AS 180Db, except:
Engine: Type OM621 4-cyl diesel, 87mm bore × 83.6mm stroke, 1,988cc. Compression ratio 21:1. 3-bearing crankshaft. Maximum power 48bhp DIN at 3,800rpm; maximum torque 80lb/ft at 2,200rpm.
Brakes: Larger swept area, as 180b.

190, produced March 1956 – August 1959 (W121)
As 180, except:
Engine: Type M121 4-cyl, 85mm bore × 83.6mm stroke, 1,897cc OHC. Compression ratio 7.5:1. 3-bearing crankshaft. Solex 32 PAITA downdraught carburettor. Maximum power 75bhp DIN at 4,600rpm; maximum torque 101lb/ft at 2,800rpm.
Transmission: Axle ratio 4.1:1.
Running gear: Single-pivot swing-axle rear suspension with coil springs. Larger brake swept area (as 180b), servo assistance optional.
Dimensions: Front track 56.3in. Weight 2,728lb.

190b, produced June 1959 – August 1961 (W121)
As 190, except:
Engine: Maximum power 80bhp DIN at 4,800rpm; maximum torque 103lb/ft at 2,800rpm.
Dimensions: Length 177.2in.

190D, produced August 1958 – July 1959 (W121)
As 190, except:
Engine: Type OM621 4-cyl, diesel, 85mm bore × 83.6mm stroke, 1,897cc OHC. Compression ratio 21:1. 3-bearing crankshaft. Maximum power 50bhp DIN at 4,000rpm; maximum torque 79.5lb/ft at 2,200rpm.
Transmission: Axle ratio 3.7:1.
Weight: 2,750lb.

190Db, produced June 1959 – September 1961 (W121)
As 190D, except:
Dimensions: Length 177.2in.

219, produced March 1956 – July 1959 (W105)
Construction: All-steel unitary body with separate front subframe.
Engine: Type M180 6-cyl, 80mm bore × 72.8mm stroke, 2,195cc OHC. Compression ratio 7.6:1 (8.7:1 from August 1957). 4-bearing crankshaft. Solex 32 PAATJ dual downdraught carburettor. Maximum power 85bhp DIN at 4,800rpm (90bhp from August 1957), maximum torque 116lb/ft at 2,400rpm (123lb/ft from August 1957).
Transmission: 4-speed all-synchromesh gearbox with reverse. Gear ratios 3.52:1, 2.32:1, 1.52:1, 1.00:1, reverse 3.29:1. Axle ratio 4.1:1 (3.9:1 from August 1957). Hydrak automatic clutch optionally available.
Running gear: Independent front suspension with coil springs; single-pivot swing-axle rear suspension with coil springs. Recirculating-ball steering, 21.4:1 ratio. Hydraulic drum brakes on all 4 wheels. 6.40 × 13 tyres.
Dimensions: Wheelbase 108.3in, front track 56.3in, rear track 57.9in, length 184.3in, width 68.5in, height 61.4in, ground clearance 7.3in. Weight 2,838lb. Turning circle 38ft.

220a, pilot-build March 1954, produced June 1954 – April 1956 (W180)
As 219, except:
Transmission: 1st gear ratio 3.40:1, later 3.52:1. Axle ratio 4.11:1, later 4.10:1.

Dimensions: Wheelbase 111in, length 185.6in. Weight 2,860lb.

220S, produced March 1956 – August 1959 (saloon); produced July 1956 – October 1959 (cabriolet); produced October 1956 – October 1959 (coupe) (W180)
As later 220a, except:
Engine: 2 Solex 32 PAJTA carburettors. Maximum power 100bhp DIN at 4,800rpm (106bhp at 5,200rpm from August 1957); maximum torque 119lb/ft at 3,500rpm (127lb/ft from August 1957).
Running gear: Servo-assisted brakes standard. 6.70 × 13 tyres.
Dimensions: Wheelbase 111in (saloon), 106.3in (coupe and cabriolet), length 187in (saloon), 183.9in (coupe and cabriolet), width 68.5in (saloon), 69.5in (coupe and cabriolet), height 61.4in (saloon), 60.2in (coupe and cabriolet). Weight 2,970lb (saloon), 3,102lb (coupe), 3,219lb (cabriolet). Turning circle 38ft (saloon), 37ft (coupe and cabriolet).

220SE, pilot-build April 1958, produced October 1958 – August 1959 (saloon); pilot-build July 1958, produced October 1958 – November 1960 (coupe and cabriolet) (W128)
As contemporary 220S, except:
Engine: Bosch fuel injection. Maximum power 115bhp DIN at 4,800rpm (120bhp from August 1959); maximum torque 152lb/ft at 4,100rpm.
Transmission: Gear ratios, US-market cars only: 3.65:1, 2.36:1, 1.53:1, 1.00:1.
Weight: 3,014lb (saloon), 3,146lb (coupe), 3,234lb (cabriolet).

190SL, pilot-build January 1955, produced May 1955 – February 1963 (W121)
Construction: All-steel unitary body with separate front subframe.
Engine: Type M121B 4-cyl, 85mm bore × 83.6mm stroke, 1,897cc OHC. Compression ratio 8.5:1 (8.7:1 from August 1957, 8.8:1 from September 1959). 3-bearing crankshaft. 2 Solex 44 PHH dual downdraught carburettors. Maximum power 105bhp DIN at 5,700rpm; maximum torque 105lb/ft at 3,200rpm.
Transmission: 4-speed all-synchromesh gearbox with reverse. Gear ratios 3.52:1, 2.32:1, 1.52:1, 1.00:1, reverse 3.29:1. Axle ratio 3.7:1 (changed very early to 3.9:1, 4.1:1 optional).
Running gear: Independent front suspension with coil springs and telescopic dampers; single-pivot swing-axle rear suspension with coil springs and telescopic dampers. Recirculating-ball steering, 18.5:1 ratio. Hydraulic Alfin drum brakes on all 4 wheels with optional vacuum servo assistance (servo standardized for 1957). 6.40 × 13 tyres.
Dimensions: Wheelbase 94.5in, front track 56.2in, rear track 58.1in, length 166.1in, width 68.5in, height 52in, ground clearance 7.3in. Weight 2,552lb (roadster), 2,596lb (coupe). Turning circle 36.1ft.

Chassis number sequences and production figures

Chassis number sequences and production figures

During the period covered by this book, 4 different chassis numbering systems have been employed on Mercedes-Benz cars:

1946-1950

11 digit numbers, broken down as follows:
First 3 numbers: Type (as W number)
Next 3 numbers: Body type (*e.g.* saloon, cabriolet, *etc.*)
Final 5 numbers: Serial number

1951-1952

13 digit numbers, as 1946-1950, but:
Last 2 numbers: Production year (*e.g.* 51 = 1951).

1953-1959

14 digit (LHD) and 15 digit (RHD) numbers, broken down as follows:
1st digit: R (RHD models only; LHD models have no identifying prefix)
Next 3 digits: Type (as W number)
Next 3 digits: Body type
Next digit: N (standard transmission) or Z (Hydrak clutch)
Next 2 digits: Production year in reverse (*e.g.* 35 = 1953, *etc*)
Final 5 digits: Serial number.

1960 and later

14 digit numbers, broken down as follows:
First 3 digits: Type (as W number)
Next 3 digits: Body type
Next digit: 1 (LHD) or 2 (RHD)
Next digit: 0 (standard transmission), 1 (Hydrak clutch), or 2 (automatic)
Final 6 digits: Serial number.

Type and body type numbers

Model by model, these numbers list out as follows:

W136 models (170V, Va, Vb, D, Da, Db, S, S-V and S-D)

	170V	170D	170S	170Va/ Vb	170Da/ Db	170S-V	170S-D
Saloon	136.010	136.110	136.040	136.060	136.160	136.081	136.181
Saloon w/sunroof	–	–·–	136.049	136.072	136.172	136.082	136.182
Cabriolet A	–	–	136.042	–	–	–	–
Cabriolet B	–	–	136.043	–	–	–	–
Ambulance	136.014	136.114	136.044	136.070	136.170	136.083	136.183
Delivery van	–	–	136.046	–	–	–	–
Pick-up	136.016	136.115	–	136.074	136.175	–	–
Police patrol car	136.017	–	136.047	–	136.174	–	–
Police radio car	–	–	136.048	–	–	–	136.187
Ditto w/sunroof	–	–	136.050	–	–	–	136.188
Taxi	136.019	–	–	136.069	136.169	–	136.184

W191 models (170Sb and 170DS)

	170Sb	170DS
Saloon	191.010	191.110
Saloon w/sunroof	191.018	191.113
Ambulance	191.013	191.111
Delivery van	–	191.112
Police patrol car	191.015	191.116
Police radio car	191.016	–
Ditto w/sunroof	191.017	–

W187 models (220)

Saloon	187.010
Cabriolet A	187.012
Cabriolet B	187.013
Saloon w/sunroof	187.014
Police radio car	187.017
Police patrol car	187.018
Coupe	187.020

W186 models (300, 300b, 300c)

	300/300b	300c
Saloon	186.000	186.016
Cabriolet B	186.013	–
Cabriolet D	186.014	186.033
Saloon w/sunroof	186.015	186.017

W189 models (300d)

Saloon	189.010
Saloon w/sunroof	189.011
Cabriolet D	189.033

W188 models (300S, 300Sc)

	300S	300Sc
Cabriolet A	188.000	188.013
Coupe	188.011	188.014
Roadster	188.012	188.015

W198 models (300SL)

Coupe	198.040
Roadster	198.042

W120 models (180, 180D; all suffix letters)

	180	180D
Saloon	120.010	120.110
Ambulance, 4-door	120.000	120.100
Special body, 2-door	120.001	120.101
Special body, 4-door	120.002	120.102

W121 models (190SL, 190 and 190D; all suffix letters)

	190SL	190	190D
Coupe	121.040	–	–
Roadster	121.042	–	–
Saloon	–	121.010	121.110
Saloon w/sunroof	–	121.011	121.111
Ambulance	–	121.000	121.100
Special body	–	121.002	121.102

W105 models (219)

Saloon	105.010
Saloon w/sunroof	105.011
Ambulance	105.000

W180 models (220a, 220S)

	220a	220S
Saloon	180.010	180.010
Saloon w/sunroof	180.011	180.011
Ambulance	180.000	180.000
Cabriolet	–	180.030
Coupe	–	180.037

W128 models (220SE)

Saloon	128.010
Saloon w/sunroof	128.011
Cabriolet	128.030
Coupe	128.037

Production totals

Note: Figures are for calendar year, not model-year.

170 models

Year	170V	170D	170S	170S Cabriolet	170Va	170Da	170DS	170Sb	170Vb
1946	214								
1947	1,045								
1948	5,116								
1949	13,101	907	3,370	39					
1950	(+)	5,609	14,735	1,686	11,876 (+)				
1951			10,333	708	12,687	14,622			
1952			326		3,692	8,115	6,734	4,580	
1953							6,251	3,514	1,636
Total	19,476 (+)	6,516	28,764	2,433	28,255 (+)	22,737	12,985	8,094	1,636

Year	170Db	170S-V	170S-D	Annual total
1946				214
1947				1,045
1948				5,116
1949				17,417
1950				33,906
1951				38,350
1952				23,447
1953	4,570	2,102	6,494	24,567
1954		880	5,992	6,872
1955		140	2,401	2,541
Total	4,570	3,122	14,887	153,475

Notes: (+) The figure of 11,876 for 170Va production in 1950 also includes those 170V models built between January and May 1950. A breakdown is not available.

170V/Va/Vb production figures may be broken down as follows:

Saloon	44,251	Van	1,685
Sd	1,489	Chassis	275
Ambulance (V)	600		
Ambulance (Va/Vb)	1,067	Grand total	49,367

220 models

Year	Saloon	Coupe/Cabriolet	Annual total
1951	3,453	368	3,821
1952	9,165	1,178	10,343
1953	3,322	403	3,725
1954	214	259	473
1955		152	152
Total	16,154	2,360	18,514

300 models

Year	300/300b Saloon	300/300b Cabriolet	300c Saloon	300c Cabriolet	300d Saloon	300d Cabriolet	Annual total
1951	47	2					49
1952	2,659	262					2,921
1953	1,776	181					1,957
1954	1,185	87					1,272
1955	547	59	330	3			939
1956			885	48			933
1957			217			144	361

1958					1,165	3	1,168
1959					607	23	630
1960					581	22	603
1961					535	16	551
1962					45	1	46
Total	6,214	591	1,432	51	3,077	65	11,430

300S models

Year	300S	300Sc	Annual total
1951	2		2
1952	113		113
1953	353		353
1954	37		.37
1955	55	5	60
1956		140	140
1957		52	52
1958		3	3
Total	560	200	760

Type breakdown:

	300S	300Sc
Roadster	141	53
Cabriolet	203	49
Coupe	216	98

300SL models

Year	300SL Gullwing	300SL Roadster/Coupe	Annual total
1954	146		146
1955	867		867
1956	311		311
1957	76	554	630
1958		324	324
1959		211	211
1960		249	249
1961		250	250
1962		244	244
1963		26	26
Total	1,400	1,858	3,258

180, 180D, 190 and 190D models

Year	180	180a	180D	180b	180Db	180c	180Dc	Annual total
1953	4,362		11					4,373
1954	20,306		15,532					35,838
1955	17,704		20,345					38,049
1956	8,464		21,013					29,477
1957	1,350	4,656	22,910					28,916
1958		15,967	26,693					42,660
1959		6,730	9,981	7,314	8,076			32,101
1960				14,384	11,151			25,535
1961				7,717	5,449	4,980	4,822	22,968
1962						4,300	7,000	11,300
Total	52,186	27,353	116,485	29,415	24,676	9,280	11,822	271,217

Year	190	190D	190b	190Db	Annual total
1956	16,001				16,001
1957	22,578				22,578
1958	15,791	5,469			21,260
1959	6,975	15,160	6,613	13,709	42,457
1960		12,986		29,116	42,102
1961			8,864	18,464	27,328
Total	61,345	20,629	28,463	61,309	171,746

220, 220S and 220SE models

Year	220a	220S	220S Cabrio/Coupe	219	220SE	220SE Cabrio/Coupe	Annual total
1954	4,178						4,178
1955	19,348						19,348
1956	2,411	10,525	297	5,474			18,707
1957		15,459	1,066	8,505			25,030
1958		20,181	1,280	9,296	201	114	31,072
1959		9,114	786	4,570	1,773	628	16,871
1960						1,200	1,200
Total	25,937	55,279	3,429	27,845	1,974	1,942	116,406

Overall totals, Ponton models

Year	4-cylinder	6-cylinder	Total
1953	4,373		4,373
1954	35,838	4,178	40,016
1955	38,049	19,348	57,397
1956	45,478	18,707	64,185
1957	51,494	25,030	76,524
1958	63,920	31,072	94,992
1959	74,558	16,871	91,429
1960	67,637	1,200	68,837
1961	50,316		50,316
1962	11,300		11,300
		Grand total	559,369

190SL models

Year	Total		Year	Total
1955	1,727		1960	3,977
1956	4,032		1961	3,792
1957	3,332		1962	2,246
1958	2,722		1963	104
1959	3,949			
			Grand total	25,881

APPENDIX C
How fast? How economical? How heavy?

Performance figures for early postwar Mercedes-Benz cars

	170D	170S saloon	220 saloon	300	180	220a	220S saloon	220S saloon with Hydrak clutch	300SL gullwing (3.64 axle)	300SL roadster (3.89 axle)	190SL
Mean maximum speed (mph)	68.8	77.2	91.8	102.8	76.3	98.9	101	101.8	135.0	125.0	106.3
Acceleration (sec)											
0-30mph	10.5	6.5	4.7	4.3	7.0	4.9	4.3	5.5	3.5	2.7	4.0
0-40mph	17.8	10.5	9.2	7.0	12.2	7.2	7.7	8.7	–	4.3	6.2
0-50mph	32.5	19.4	14.7	10.4	18.7	11.7	11.2	12.8	7.0	5.9	8.6
0-60mph	47.6	29.0	19.5	14.9	29.5	15.1	15.2	16.9	8.8	7.8	11.2
0-70mph	–	–	28.8	19.9	–	22.1	20.2	21.6	11.0	10.6	16.2
0-80mph	–	–	40.2	26.9	–	32.2	28.0	31.8	13.8	12.8	23.0
0-90mph	–	–	–	38.2	–	52.0	36.0	44.5	16.1	15.4	–
0-100mph	–	–	–	–	–	–	42.4	–	21.0	19.2	–
Standing ¼-mile (sec)	26.8	25.0	21.4	19.9	23.4	20.1	20.4	21.2	16.1	16.3	18.2
Direct top gear (sec)											
10-30mph	17.5	15.0	12.8	11.2	16.8	10.1	–	9.8	–	–	–
20-40mph	19.5	14.9	12.5	11.3	16.0	9.1	–	10.8	7.8	–	–
30-50mph	20.0	16.1	11.2	11.0	16.6	8.8	–	10.3	7.9	–	–
40-60mph	29.8	19.8	11.7	11.1	20.5	9.5	–	10.2	7.8	–	–
50-70mph	–	–	13.8	11.5	–	12.3	–	12.7	7.5	–	–
60-80mph	–	–	29.3	11.8	–	16.7	–	17.8	8.0	–	–
70-90mph	–	–	–	17.0	–	29.3	–	20.9	–	–	–
80-100mph	–	–	–	–	–	–	–	–	8.2	–	–
Overall fuel consumption (mpg)	over 40	23.7	18.9	16.2	26.7	21.0	–	22.5	18.4	–	approx 25
Typical fuel consumption (mpg)	–	–	–	–	–	–	24.5	23.8	15-23	21.3	–
Kerb weight (cwt)	24.1	25.4	26.5	35.4	22	26	26.3	25.9	24.5	27.6*	25.7
Original test published	*Motor* July 12 1950	*Motor* June 28 1950	*Motor* November 21 1951	*Motor* April 23 1952	*Motor* June 23 1954	*Motor* June 22 1955	*Sports Cars Illustrated* November 1956	*Motor* December 4 1957	*Autocar* March 25 1955	*Sports Cars Illustrated* December 1957	*Autosport* November 11 1955

*with full tank of fuel